Introduction

Birthdays hold a unique magic in our lives. They mark the passage of time, encapsulating memories, hopes, and dreams within the framework of a single day. The anniversary of our birth is a personal milestone that connects us to our past, present, and future. But have you ever wondered about the wider world of people who share your special day? Who else came into the world on the very day you did? What iconic figures, trailblazers, and artists share that same cosmic alignment?

In "More than Balloons: Your Celebrity Birthday Buds" We embark on a captivating journey through the calendar, exploring the lives of five famous individuals born on each day of the year. From January 1st to December 31st, we unravel the stories of visionaries, creators, leaders, and entertainers who've left their indelible mark on history. As you delve into this book, you'll discover that you're not just celebrating your birthday; you're joining a legacy of individuals who've contributed to the rich tapestry of human experience.

Imagine the conversations you could have with these icons if you were to meet them at a cosmic birthday party. What wisdom would Martin Luther King Jr. share on January 15th? How might sharing a birthday with Albert Einstein or Amelia Earhart influence your perspective on March 14th? And what about the dynamic duo of John Lennon and Bruce Lee, both born on October 9th? The connections become limitless, and the stories intertwine to reveal the breadth of human achievement and potential.

Each day of the year holds a universe of stories waiting to be explored. From actors to scientists, musicians to athletes, political leaders to artists, this book brings you face to face with the extraordinary individuals who have made their mark on the world. With every turn of the page, you'll be greeted by a new cast of characters, each bound to your birthday by fate, circumstance, and the rhythm of the universe.

The purpose of "More than Balloons: Your Celebrity Birthday Buds?" is to celebrate the beauty of connections across time and space. It's a tribute to the idea that our birthdays not only belong to us but are also shared with people who have shaped the world in profound ways. As you read through these pages, you'll not only learn about the lives of influential figures but also gain a deeper understanding of the significance of your own birthday. So, let's embark on this captivating journey together, exploring the extraordinary lives that share a date with your own.

January Birthdays

January 1st

·   **Paul Revere (1735)** - American silversmith and patriot known for his midnight ride to warn of British troops' movements during the American Revolution.

·   **J.D. Salinger (1919)** - American author famous for the novel "The Catcher in the Rye."

·   **Betsy Ross (1752)** - Seamstress credited with making the first American flag.

·   **Verne Troyer (1969)** - Actor best known for his role as Mini-Me in the "Austin Powers" films.

·   **Elin Nordegren (1980)** - Swedish model and former wife of professional golfer Tiger Woods.

January 2nd

o **Isaac Asimov (1920)** - Prolific science fiction author known for works like "Foundation" and "I, Robot."

o **Jim Bakker (1940)** - American televangelist and former host of "The PTL Club."

o **Christy Turlington (1969)** - Supermodel and women's health advocate.

o **Taye Diggs (1971)** - Actor known for his roles in "Rent" and TV series like "Private Practice."

o **Kate Bosworth (1983)** - Actress recognized for her performances in movies like "Blue Crush" and "Superman Returns."

January 3rd

§ **J.R.R. Tolkien (1892)** - English author known for creating the fantasy world of Middle-earth in "The Lord of the Rings" series.

§ **Mel Gibson (1956)** - Actor and filmmaker famous for his roles in "Braveheart" and "Lethal Weapon" series.

§ **Michael Schumacher (1969)** - German Formula One racing driver, considered one of the greatest in the sport.

§ **Dan Harmon (1973)** - Creator of the TV series "Community" and co-creator of "Rick and Morty."

§ **Eli Manning (1981)** - Former NFL quarterback, best known for leading the New York Giants to two Super Bowl victories.

January 4th

v **Louis Braille (1809) -** French educator who developed the Braille system for the blind.

v **Sir Isaac Newton (1643)** - Renowned physicist and mathematician known for his laws of motion and universal gravitation.

v **Michael Stipe (1960**) - Lead vocalist of the rock band R.E.M.

v **Julia Ormond (1965)** - British actress known for roles in "Legends of the Fall" and "Sabrina."

v **Chrisette Michele (1982)** - R&B and soul singer-songwriter.

January 5th

Ø **Marilyn Manson (1969)** - Controversial American singer, songwriter, and actor known for his provocative stage presence.

Ø **Bradley Cooper (1975)** - Actor and filmmaker recognized for his roles in "Silver Linings Playbook" and "American Sniper."

Ø **Robert Duvall (1931)** - Veteran actor acclaimed for performances in "The Godfather" and "Apocalypse Now."

Ø **Diane Keaton (1946)** - Actress and film director known for her roles in Woody Allen films and "Annie Hall."

Ø **Deepika Padukone (1986)** - Indian actress and producer, one of the highest-paid actresses in India.

January 6th

ü **Joan of Arc (1412)** - French military leader and martyr during the Hundred Years' War.

ü **Eddie Redmayne (1982)** - British actor known for his roles in "The Theory of Everything" and the "Fantastic Beasts" series.

ü **Norman Reedus (1969)** - Actor famous for portraying Daryl Dixon in the TV series "The Walking Dead."

ü **Rowan Atkinson (1955)** - English comedian and actor, best known for his character Mr. Bean.

ü **Kate McKinnon (1984)** - Comedian and actress, a cast member on "Saturday Night Live."

January 7th

· **Nicolas Cage (1964)** - Actor known for his diverse roles in films like "Leaving Las Vegas" and "National Treasure."

· **Zora Neale Hurston (1891)** - African American author and anthropologist, celebrated for her novel "Their Eyes Were Watching God."

· **Katie Couric (1957)** - Journalist and TV host known for her work on "Today" and the "CBS Evening News."

· **Jeremy Renner (1971)** - Actor recognized for his performances in the "Avengers" films and "The Hurt Locker."

· **Lauren Cohan (1982)** - Actress known for her role as Maggie Greene on the TV series "The Walking Dead."

January 8th

o **Elvis Presley (1935)** - The "King of Rock and Roll," one of the most influential musicians of the 20th century.

o **Stephen Hawking (1942)** - Theoretical physicist known for his work on black holes and cosmology.

o **David Bowie (1947)** - Iconic British musician and actor renowned for his innovative music and alter egos.

o **R. Kelly (1967)** - Controversial R&B singer, songwriter, and producer.

o **Gaby Hoffmann (1982)** - Actress known for her roles in films like "Field of Dreams" and the TV series "Transparent."

January 9th

§ **Richard Nixon (1913)** - 37th President of the United States, known for the Watergate scandal.

§ **Dave Matthews (1967)** - Musician and frontman of the Dave Matthews Band.

§ **Kate Middleton (1982)** - Duchess of Cambridge and wife of Prince William, Duke of Cambridge.

§ **Nina Dobrev (1989)** - Bulgarian-Canadian actress recognized for her role in the TV series "The Vampire Diaries."

§ **Joey Lauren Adams (1968)** - Actress known for her roles in "Chasing Amy" and "Dazed and Confused."

January 10th

v **Rod Stewart (1945)** - British rock singer-songwriter known for hits like "Maggie May" and "Do Ya Think I'm Sexy?"

v **Pat Benatar (1953)** - American rock singer recognized for songs like "Love Is a Battlefield" and "Hit Me with Your Best Shot."

v **Jim Croce (1943)** - American folk singer-songwriter known for hits such as "Bad, Bad Leroy Brown" and "Time in a Bottle."

v **Hrithik Roshan (1974)** - Indian actor and one of the highest-paid actors in Bollywood.

v **Sarah Shahi (1980)** - Actress known for her roles in TV series like "Person of Interest" and "The L Word."

January 11th

Ø **Alexander Hamilton (1755)** - Founding Father of the United States, author of Federalist Papers, and first Secretary of the Treasury.

Ø **Mary J. Blige (1971)** - Grammy-winning R&B singer-songwriter known for hits like "Real Love" and "No More Drama."

Ø **Naomi Judd (1946)** - American country music singer and member of the duo The Judds.

Ø **Amanda Peet (1972)** - Actress recognized for roles in "The Whole Nine Yards" and "Studio 60 on the Sunset Strip."

Ø **Jason Segel (1980)** - Actor known for his role in the TV series "How I Met Your Mother" and the film "Forgetting Sarah Marshall."

January 12th

ü **Jack London (1876)** - American novelist and journalist best known for "The Call of the Wild" and "White Fang."

ü **Kirstie Alley (1951)** - Actress known for her roles in "Cheers" and "Look Who's Talking."

ü **Jeff Bezos (1964)** - Founder of Amazon, entrepreneur, and space enthusiast.

ü **Rachael Harris (1968)** - Actress and comedian recognized for her work in "The Hangover" films and TV series like "Suits."

ü **Zayn Malik (1993)** - English singer and former member of the boy band One Direction.

January 13th

· **Patrick Dempsey (1966)** - Actor known for his role as Dr. Derek Shepherd on the TV series "Grey's Anatomy."

· **Orlando Bloom (1977)** - British actor recognized for his roles in "Pirates of the Caribbean" and "The Lord of the Rings" series.

· **Julia Louis-Dreyfus (1961)** - Actress famous for her roles in "Seinfeld" and "Veep."

· **Liam Hemsworth (1990)** - Australian actor known for his roles in "The Hunger Games" series and "The Last Song."

· **Penelope Ann Miller (1964)** - Actress known for her roles in "Carlito's Way" and "The Artist."

January 14th

o **LL Cool J (1968)** - Rapper and actor known for hits like "Mama Said Knock You Out" and his role on "NCIS: Los Angeles."

o **Faye Dunaway (1941)** - Actress acclaimed for her roles in "Bonnie and Clyde" and "Network."

o **Grant Gustin (1990)** - Actor recognized for his portrayal of Barry Allen in the TV series "The Flash."

o **Jason Bateman (1969)** - Actor known for his roles in "Arrested Development" and "Ozark."

o **Dave Grohl (1969)** - Musician and lead vocalist of the rock band Foo Fighters, formerly drummer for Nirvana.

January 15th

§ **Martin Luther King Jr. (1929)** - Civil rights leader and activist known for his role in the American civil rights movement.

§ **Pitbull (1981)** - American rapper and musician known for hits like "Timber" and "Give Me Everything."

§ **Regina King (1971)** - Actress recognized for her roles in "Jerry Maguire" and TV series like "Southland" and "Watchmen."

§ **Drew Brees (1979)** - Retired NFL quarterback, known for leading the New Orleans Saints to victory in Super Bowl XLIV.

§ **Dove Cameron (1996)** - Actress and singer known for her roles in Disney Channel shows and the film "Descendants."

January 16th

v **Aaliyah (1979)** - Singer, actress, and model known for her R&B hits and roles in films like "Romeo Must Die."

v **Lin-Manuel Miranda (1980)** - Playwright, composer, and actor, creator of the musicals "Hamilton" and "In the Heights."

v **Kate Moss (1974)** - British supermodel known for her work with various fashion brands.

v **John Carpenter (1948)** - Filmmaker, screenwriter, and composer, known for directing horror classics like "Halloween" and "The Thing."

v **Ethel Merman (1908)** - Broadway actress and singer known for her powerful voice and roles in musicals like "Annie Get Your Gun."

January 17th

Ø **Muhammad Ali (1942)** - Legendary boxer and cultural icon, considered one of the greatest athletes of all time.

Ø **Zooey Deschanel (1980)** - Actress known for her roles in "New Girl" and films like "(500) Days of Summer."

Ø **Jim Carrey (1962)** - Actor and comedian famous for roles in "Ace Ventura: Pet Detective" and "The Truman Show."

Ø **Michelle Obama (1964)** - Lawyer, author, and former First Lady of the United States, focused on education and health issues.

Ø **Betty White (1922)** - Legendary actress known for her roles in "The Golden Girls" and numerous other TV shows.

January 18th

ü **Kevin Costner (1955)** - Actor, director, and producer known for films like "Dances with Wolves" and "Field of Dreams."

ü **Jason Segel (1980)** - Actor and comedian recognized for his roles in "Forgetting Sarah Marshall" and "How I Met Your Mother."

ü **Dave Bautista (1969)** - Former professional wrestler turned actor known for his role as Drax in the "Guardians of the Galaxy" films.

ü **Mary Oliver (1935)** - Influential American poet known for her contemplative and nature-focused work.

ü **Joanna Newsom (1982)** - Singer-songwriter and harpist known for her unique musical style and albums like "Ys."

January 19th

·   **Dolly Parton (1946)** - Country music icon, singer, and songwriter known for hits like "Jolene" and "9 to 5."

·   **Janis Joplin (1943)** - Legendary rock singer known for her powerful vocals and hits like "Piece of My Heart."

·   **Edgar Allan Poe (1809)** - American writer and poet known for his dark and macabre tales like "The Raven" and "The Tell-Tale Heart."

·   **Katey Sagal (1954)** - Actress known for her roles in "Married... with Children" and "Sons of Anarchy."

·   **Logan Lerman (1992)** - Actor known for his roles in the "Percy Jackson" film series and "The Perks of Being a Wallflower."

January 20th

o **David Lynch (1946)** - Filmmaker and artist known for his surreal and enigmatic works like "Twin Peaks" and "Blue Velvet."

o **Buzz Aldrin (1930)** - Astronaut and engineer, second person to walk on the Moon during the Apollo 11 mission.

o **Rainn Wilson (1966)** - Actor recognized for his role as Dwight Schrute on the TV series "The Office."

o **Evan Peters (1987)** - Actor known for his roles in various seasons of the TV series "American Horror Story."

o **Skeet Ulrich (1970)** - Actor known for his roles in "Scream" and TV series like "Riverdale."

January 21st

§ **Christian Dior (1905)** - French fashion designer who founded the iconic fashion house Dior.

§ **Geena Davis (1956)** - Actress known for her roles in "Thelma & Louise" and "A League of Their Own."

§ **Emma Bunton (1976)** - British singer and member of the girl group Spice Girls, known as "Baby Spice."

§ **Plácido Domingo (1941)** - Spanish opera singer and conductor, one of the most renowned tenors in the world.

§ **Jerry Trainor (1977)** - Actor known for his role as Spencer Shay on the TV series "iCarly."

January 22nd

v **Diane Lane (1965)** - Actress recognized for roles in "Unfaithful" and "Under the Tuscan Sun."

v **Guy Fieri (1968)** - Celebrity chef and TV host known for "Diners, Drive-Ins and Dives."

v **John Hurt (1940)** - English actor known for his roles in "The Elephant Man" and "Alien."

v **Sam Cooke (1931)** - Influential American singer-songwriter known for hits like "A Change Is Gonna Come" and "You Send Me."

v **Linda Blair (1959)** - Actress known for her role in the horror film "The Exorcist."

January 23rd

Ø **Arjen Robben (1984)** - Dutch former professional footballer known for his time with clubs like Bayern Munich.

Ø **Rutger Hauer (1944)** - Dutch actor known for his roles in "Blade Runner" and "The Hitcher."

Ø **Mariska Hargitay (1964)** - Actress recognized for her role as Olivia Benson on the TV series "Law & Order: SVU."

Ø **Tiffani Thiessen (1974)** - Actress known for her roles in "Saved by the Bell" and "Beverly Hills, 90210."

Ø **Julia Jones (1981)** - Actress of Choctaw and Chickasaw descent known for her roles in the "Twilight" series and TV series like "Westworld."

January 24th

ü **Neil Diamond (1941)** - Singer-songwriter known for hits like "Sweet Caroline" and "I Am... I Said."

ü **Mary Lou Retton (1968)** - Olympic gymnast and gold medalist in the 1984 Summer Olympics.

ü **Mischa Barton (1986)** - Actress recognized for her role as Marissa Cooper on the TV series "The O.C."

ü **Ed Helms (1974)** - Actor and comedian known for his roles in "The Hangover" films and "The Office."

ü **Ricky Ullman (1986)** - Actor known for his role in the Disney Channel series "Phil of the Future."

January 25th

· **Robert Burns (1759)** - Scottish poet and lyricist, known for works like "Auld Lang Syne" and "Tam o' Shanter."

· **Alicia Keys (1981)** - Singer-songwriter known for her soulful voice and hits like "Fallin'" and "No One."

· **Virginia Woolf (1882)** - English writer and modernist, famous for novels like "Mrs. Dalloway" and "To the Lighthouse."

· **Dean Jones (1931)** - Actor known for his roles in Disney films like "The Love Bug" and "That Darn Cat!"

· **Ana Ortiz (1971)** - Actress recognized for her roles in the TV series "Ugly Betty" and "Devious Maids."

January 26th

o **Ellen DeGeneres (1958)** - Comedian, actress, and TV host known for "The Ellen DeGeneres Show."

o **Wayne Gretzky (1961)** - Legendary Canadian ice hockey player widely regarded as one of the greatest.

o **Paul Newman (1925)** - Acclaimed actor, philanthropist, and co-founder of Newman's Own food company.

o **Eddie Van Halen (1955)** - Influential guitarist and co-founder of the rock band Van Halen.

o **Portia de Rossi (1973)** - Actress known for her roles in TV series like "Ally McBeal" and "Arrested Development."

January 27th

§ **Wolfgang Amadeus Mozart (1756)** - Renowned composer of the classical era, known for symphonies, operas, and more.

§ **Lewis Carroll (1832)** - English author and mathematician known for his novels "Alice's Adventures in Wonderland" and "Through the Looking-Glass."

§ **Bridget Fonda (1964)** - Actress known for her roles in "Single White Female" and "Jackie Brown."

§ **Patton Oswalt (1969)** - Comedian and actor known for his stand-up comedy and roles in TV series like "The King of Queens."

§ **Rosamund Pike (1979)** - British actress recognized for her roles in "Gone Girl" and "Pride & Prejudice."

January 28th

v **Alan Alda (1936)** - Actor, director, and writer known for his role as Hawkeye Pierce on the TV series "MAS*H."

v **Elijah Wood (1981)** - Actor recognized for his role as Frodo Baggins in "The Lord of the Rings" film series.

v **Nick Carter (1980)** - Singer and member of the Backstreet Boys, one of the best-selling music groups.

v **Ariel Winter (1998)** - Actress known for her role as Alex Dunphy on the TV series "Modern Family."

v **Jackson Pollock (1912)** - Influential American painter and a major figure in the abstract expressionist movement.

January 29th

Ø **Oprah Winfrey (1954)** - Media mogul, television host, and philanthropist known for "The Oprah Winfrey Show."

Ø **Tom Selleck (1945)** - Actor recognized for his role in the TV series "Magnum, P.I." and films like "Three Men and a Baby."

Ø **Heather Graham (1970)** - Actress known for her roles in "Boogie Nights" and "The Hangover" series.

Ø **Adam Lambert (1982)** - Singer-songwriter and former "American Idol" contestant, known for his powerful vocals.

Ø **Sara Gilbert (1975)** - Actress known for her roles in TV series like "Roseanne" and "The Conners."

January 30th

ü **Franklin D. Roosevelt (1882)** - 32nd President of the United States, led the nation through the Great Depression and WWII.

ü **Gene Hackman (1930)** - Acclaimed actor known for roles in "The French Connection" and "Unforgiven."

ü **Phil Lester (1987)** - British YouTuber and former radio presenter known for his online content and collaborations.

ü **Christian Bale (1974)** - Actor recognized for his roles in "The Dark Knight" trilogy and "American Psycho."

ü **Vanessa Redgrave (1937)** - British actress known for her roles in films like "Julia" and "Atonement."

January 31st

·   **Justin Timberlake (1981)** - Singer-songwriter, actor, and former member of *NSYNC, known for hits like "Cry Me a River" and "SexyBack."

·   **Jackie Robinson (1919)** - Baseball legend, the first African American to play in Major League Baseball in the modern era.

·   **Kerry Washington (1977)** - Actress recognized for her roles in TV series like "Scandal" and films like "Django Unchained."

·   **Portia de Rossi (1973)** - Actress known for her roles in TV series like "Ally McBeal" and "Arrested Development."

·   **Minnie Driver (1970)** - Actress known for her roles in films like "Good Will Hunting" and "The Phantom of the Opera."

February Birthdays

February 1st

· **Clark Gable (1901)** - Iconic American actor known for his role as Rhett Butler in "Gone with the Wind."

· **Harry Styles (1994)** - British singer-songwriter and former member of the boy band One Direction.

· **Langston Hughes (1902)** - Influential American poet, social activist, and a key figure of the Harlem Renaissance.

· **Lisa Marie Presley (1968)** - Singer-songwriter and daughter of Elvis Presley.

· **Sherilyn Fenn (1965)** - Actress known for her role as Audrey Horne in the TV series "Twin Peaks."

February 2nd

o **James Joyce (1882)** - Irish novelist and poet renowned for his masterpiece "Ulysses."

o **Shakira (1977)** - Colombian singer-songwriter known for hits like "Hips Don't Lie" and "Whenever, Wherever."

o **Christie Brinkley (1954)** - Model and actress recognized for her appearances in the Sports Illustrated Swimsuit Issue.

o **Gemma Arterton (1986)** - British actress known for roles in "Quantum of Solace" and "Prince of Persia."

o **Farrah Fawcett (1947)** - Actress and model known for her iconic role in the TV series "Charlie's Angels."

February 3rd

§ **Norman Rockwell (1894)** - American painter and illustrator known for his depictions of everyday life.

§ **Isla Fisher (1976)** - Actress recognized for roles in "Wedding Crashers" and "Confessions of a Shopaholic."

§ **Daddy Yankee (1977)** - Puerto Rican singer, songwriter, and rapper known for popularizing reggaeton music.

§ **Blythe Danner (1943)** - Actress known for her roles in films like "Meet the Parents" and "The Great Santini."

§ **Warwick Davis (1970)** - Actor known for roles in "Willow," "Star Wars," and the "Harry Potter" series.

February 4th

v **Rosa Parks (1913)** - Civil rights activist who famously refused to give up her bus seat, sparking the Montgomery Bus Boycott.

v **Alice Cooper (1948)** - Rock singer known for theatrical performances and hits like "School's Out."

v **Natalie Imbruglia (1975)** - Australian singer-songwriter and actress known for her hit "Torn."

v **Gabrielle Anwar (1970)** - English-American actress recognized for her roles in "Scent of a Woman" and "Burn Notice."

v **Clint Black (1962)** - Country music singer-songwriter known for songs like "Killin' Time" and "A Better Man."

February 5th

Ø **Cristiano Ronaldo (1985)** - Portuguese professional footballer widely regarded as one of the greatest of all time.

Ø **Laura Linney (1964)** - Actress known for her roles in "The Truman Show" and TV series like "Ozark."

Ø **Bobby Brown (1969)** - Singer-songwriter and dancer known for hits like "My Prerogative" and "Every Little Step."

Ø **Michael Sheen (1969)** - Welsh actor recognized for roles in "Frost/Nixon" and "Masters of Sex."

Ø **Hank Aaron (1934)** - Baseball legend and Hall of Famer, known for breaking Babe Ruth's home run record.

February 6th

ü **Bob Marley (1945)** - Jamaican reggae musician and cultural icon known for songs like "No Woman, No Cry" and "One Love."

ü **Ronald Reagan (1911)** - 40th President of the United States, known for conservative policies and diplomacy with the USSR.

ü **Natalie Cole (1950)** - American singer and daughter of Nat King Cole, known for her hit "Unforgettable."

ü **Alice Eve (1982)** - British actress recognized for her roles in "Star Trek Into Darkness" and "She's Out of My League."

ü **Tom Brokaw (1940)** - Journalist and former NBC News anchor, known for covering major historical events.

February 7th

·   **Charles Dickens (1812)** - Renowned English novelist known for classics like "Great Expectations" and "A Tale of Two Cities."

·   **Ashton Kutcher (1978)** - Actor known for his roles in "That '70s Show" and films like "Dude, Where's My Car?"

·   **Chris Rock (1965)** - Comedian and actor known for his stand-up comedy and roles in films like "Grown Ups."

·   **Garth Brooks (1962)** - Country music superstar known for hits like "Friends in Low Places" and "The Dance."

·   **Laura Ingalls Wilder (1867)** - American author known for the "Little House on the Prairie" book series.

February 8th

o **John Williams (1932)** - Prolific composer known for scoring iconic films like "Star Wars," "Jurassic Park," and "E.T."

o **James Dean (1931)** - American actor known for his roles in "Rebel Without a Cause" and "East of Eden."

o **Seth Green (1974)** - Actor, comedian, and voice actor known for roles in "Buffy the Vampire Slayer" and "Family Guy."

o **Mary Steenburgen (1953)** - Actress recognized for her roles in "Back to the Future Part III" and "Melvin and Howard."

o **Nick Nolte (1941)** - Actor known for his roles in "48 Hrs." and "The Prince of Tides."

February 9th

§ **Mia Farrow (1945)** - Actress and activist known for her roles in "Rosemary's Baby" and "The Great Gatsby."

§ **Tom Hiddleston (1981)** - British actor known for his portrayal of Loki in the Marvel Cinematic Universe.

§ **Charlie Day (1976)** - Actor and comedian recognized for his role on the TV series "It's Always Sunny in Philadelphia."

§ **Travis Tritt (1963)** - Country music singer-songwriter known for hits like "T-R-O-U-B-L-E" and "Anymore."

§ **Gypsy Rose Lee (1911)** - American burlesque entertainer and memoirist.

February 10th

v **Laura Dern (1967)** - Actress known for her roles in "Jurassic Park," "Blue Velvet," and "Big Little Lies."

v **Emma Roberts (1991)** - Actress and singer known for her roles in "American Horror Story" and "Scream Queens."

v **Elizabeth Banks (1974)** - Actress known for her roles in "The Hunger Games" series and "Pitch Perfect."

v **Leontyne Price (1927)** - Acclaimed American operatic soprano known for her powerful voice and performances.

v **Chloe Grace Moretz (1997)** - Actress known for her roles in "Kick-Ass," "Let Me In," and "Carrie."

February 11th

Ø **Thomas Edison (1847)** - American inventor known for his contributions to the development of the light bulb and phonograph.

Ø **Jennifer Aniston (1969)** - Actress known for her role as Rachel Green on the TV series "Friends."

Ø **Taylor Lautner (1992)** - Actor recognized for his role as Jacob Black in the "Twilight" film series.

Ø **Sheryl Crow (1962)** - Singer-songwriter known for hits like "All I Wanna Do" and "Soak Up the Sun."

Ø **Damian Lewis (1971)** - British actor known for his roles in TV series like "Homeland" and "Billions."

February 12th

ü **Abraham Lincoln (1809)** - 16th President of the United States, known for leading the nation during the Civil War and his abolitionist efforts.

ü **Christina Ricci (1980)** - Actress recognized for her roles in films like "The Addams Family" and "Sleepy Hollow."

ü **Josh Brolin (1968)** - Actor known for his roles in "No Country for Old Men," "Avengers," and "Deadpool 2."

ü **Arsenio Hall (1956)** - Comedian, actor, and talk show host known for "The Arsenio Hall Show."

ü **Jesse Spencer (1979)** - Australian actor recognized for his role on the TV series "House."

February 13th

· **Peter Gabriel (1950)** - British musician, singer-songwriter, and co-founder of the rock band Genesis.

· **Robbie Williams (1974)** - British singer-songwriter known for his solo career and time with the group Take That.

· **Jerry Springer (1944)** - Television personality and host of "The Jerry Springer Show."

· **Kim Novak (1933)** - Actress known for her roles in films like "Vertigo" and "Picnic."

· **Henry Rollins (1961)** - Musician, actor, and spoken word artist known for his work with the punk band Black Flag.

February 14th

o **Michael Bloomberg (1942)** - Business magnate, politician, and former Mayor of New York City.

o **Freddie Highmore (1992)** - British actor recognized for his roles in "Finding Neverland" and TV series like "Bates Motel."

o **Simon Pegg (1970)** - British actor, comedian, and writer known for "Shaun of the Dead" and the "Cornetto Trilogy."

o **Meg Tilly (1960)** - Actress known for her roles in "Agnes of God" and "The Big Chill."

o **Florence Henderson (1934)** - Actress and singer best known for her role as Carol Brady on "The Brady Bunch."

February 15th

§ **Galileo Galilei (1564)** - Italian astronomer, physicist, and mathematician who played a key role in the scientific revolution.

§ **Jane Seymour (1951)** - British-American actress known for her roles in "Live and Let Die" and TV series like "Dr. Quinn, Medicine Woman."

§ **Chris Farley (1964)** - Comedian and actor known for his work on "Saturday Night Live" and films like "Tommy Boy."

§ **Amber Riley (1986)** - Actress and singer recognized for her role in the TV series "Glee."

§ **Susan B. Anthony (1820)** - American suffragette and social reformer who played a crucial role in the women's suffrage movement.

February 16th

v **John McEnroe (1959)** - Former professional tennis player known for his intense playing style and on-court antics.

v **Elizabeth Olsen (1989)** - Actress recognized for her portrayal of Scarlet Witch in the Marvel Cinematic Universe.

v **Sonny Bono (1935)** - Singer, songwriter, and politician known for his musical career and serving in Congress.

v **Ice-T (1958)** - Rapper, actor, and musician known for his role on the TV series "Law & Order: SVU."

v **Christopher Eccleston (1964)** - British actor known for his role as the Ninth Doctor in "Doctor Who."

February 17th

Ø **Michael Jordan (1963)** - Legendary NBA basketball player widely regarded as one of the greatest athletes of all time.

Ø **Paris Hilton (1981)** - Socialite, media personality, and businesswoman known for her reality TV show and various ventures.

Ø **Denise Richards (1971)** - Actress known for her roles in "Wild Things" and "Starship Troopers."

Ø **Joseph Gordon-Levitt (1981)** - Actor known for his roles in "Inception," "500 Days of Summer," and "The Dark Knight Rises."

Ø **Bonnie Wright (1991)** - British actress recognized for her portrayal of Ginny Weasley in the "Harry Potter" film series.

February 18th

ü **Toni Morrison (1931)** - Acclaimed American novelist known for works like "Beloved" and "Song of Solomon."

ü **John Travolta (1954)** - Actor known for his roles in "Grease," "Pulp Fiction," and "Saturday Night Fever."

ü **Yoko Ono (1933)** - Japanese multimedia artist and musician, known for her association with John Lennon.

ü **Matt Dillon (1964)** - Actor known for his roles in films like "The Outsiders" and "Crash."

ü **Molly Ringwald (1968)** - Actress recognized for her roles in John Hughes' films like "Sixteen Candles" and "The Breakfast Club."

February 19th

· **Smokey Robinson (1940)** - Singer, songwriter, and record producer known for his work with The Miracles and as a solo artist.

· **Victoria Justice (1993)** - Actress and singer recognized for her roles in TV shows like "Victorious" and "Zoey 101."

· **Seal (1963)** - British singer-songwriter known for his hit "Kiss from a Rose" and soulful music.

· **Millie Bobby Brown (2004)** - Actress known for her role as Eleven in the TV series "Stranger Things."

· **Benicio del Toro (1967)** - Puerto Rican actor known for his roles in "Traffic" and "Sicario."

February 20th

o **Kurt Cobain (1967)** - Musician and frontman of the grunge band Nirvana, known for his impactful contributions to music.

o **Cindy Crawford (1966)** - Model and businesswoman known for her iconic status in the fashion industry.

o **Rihanna (1988)** - Barbadian singer-songwriter, actress, and entrepreneur known for her chart-topping hits.

o **Sidney Poitier (1927)** - Actor, film director, and author known for breaking barriers as a black actor in Hollywood.

o **Ivana Trump (1949)** - Businesswoman and former wife of Donald Trump, known for her role in the Trump Organization.

February 21st

§ **Nina Simone (1933)** - American singer, songwriter, and civil rights activist known for her unique voice and powerful songs.

§ **Alan Rickman (1946)** - British actor known for his roles in "Die Hard," "Harry Potter," and "Sense and Sensibility."

§ **Sophie Turner (1996)** - British actress recognized for her portrayal of Sansa Stark in the TV series "Game of Thrones."

§ **Kelsey Grammer (1955)** - Actor known for his role as Dr. Frasier Crane on TV series like "Cheers" and "Frasier."

§ **Ellen Page (1987)** - Canadian actress known for roles in films like "Juno" and "Inception."

February 22nd

v **George Washington (1732)** - First President of the United States and one of the Founding Fathers of the nation.

v **Drew Barrymore (1975)** - Actress known for her roles in "E.T. the Extra-Terrestrial," "Never Been Kissed," and more.

v **James Blunt (1974)** - British singer-songwriter known for hits like "You're Beautiful" and "Goodbye My Lover."

v **Jeri Ryan (1968)** - Actress recognized for her role as Seven of Nine on the TV series "Star Trek: Voyager."

v **Steve Irwin (1962)** - Australian zookeeper, conservationist, and TV personality known as the "Crocodile Hunter."

February 23rd

Ø **Aziz Ansari (1983)** - Comedian, actor, and writer known for his stand-up comedy and roles in TV shows like "Parks and Recreation."

Ø **Emily Blunt (1983)** - British-American actress known for her roles in "The Devil Wears Prada," "A Quiet Place," and more.

Ø **Dakota Fanning (1994)** - Actress who gained fame as a child star and appeared in films like "War of the Worlds" and "Coraline."

Ø **Peter Fonda (1940)** - Actor known for his roles in films like "Easy Rider" and "Ulee's Gold."

Ø **Niecy Nash (1970)** - Actress and comedian recognized for her roles in TV series like "Reno 911!" and "Claws."

February 24th

ü **Steve Jobs (1955)** - Co-founder of Apple Inc. and a pioneer in the computer and technology industry.

ü **Kristin Davis (1965)** - Actress recognized for her role as Charlotte York in the TV series "Sex and the City."

ü **Floyd Mayweather Jr. (1977)** - Professional boxer considered one of the greatest of all time.

ü **Billy Zane (1966)** - Actor known for his roles in "Titanic," "The Phantom," and "Back to the Future Part II."

ü **Edward James Olmos (1947)** - Actor and director known for his roles in "Stand and Deliver" and "Battlestar Galactica."

February 25th

· **George Harrison (1943)** - British musician, singer-songwriter, and lead guitarist of The Beatles.

· **Rashida Jones (1976)** - Actress and writer known for her roles in TV series like "Parks and Recreation" and "The Office."

· **Sean Astin (1971)** - Actor recognized for his roles in "The Goonies," "The Lord of the Rings," and "Stranger Things."

· **Chelsea Handler (1975)** - Comedian, actress, and TV host known for her late-night talk show "Chelsea Lately."

· **Tea Leoni (1966)** - Actress known for her roles in "Deep Impact" and TV series like "Madam Secretary."

February 26th

o **Levi Strauss (1829)** - German-American businessman who co-founded the denim jeans company Levi Strauss & Co.

o **Erykah Badu (1971)** - American singer-songwriter known for her neo-soul music and distinctive style.

o **Johnny Cash (1932)** - Legendary American singer-songwriter known as the "Man in Black."

o **Natalia Lafourcade (1984)** - Mexican singer-songwriter known for her fusion of folk, pop, and Latin music.

o **Michael Bolton (1953)** - Singer known for his powerful voice and hits like "How Am I Supposed to Live Without You."

February 27th

§ **Elizabeth Taylor (1932)** - British-American actress known for her roles in "Cleopatra," "Who's Afraid of Virginia Woolf?," and more.

§ **Josh Groban (1981)** - Singer-songwriter known for his powerful voice and classical-pop crossover music.

§ **Kate Mara (1983)** - Actress recognized for her roles in TV series like "House of Cards" and "American Horror Story."

§ **Chelsea Clinton (1980)** - Author, journalist, and daughter of former U.S. President Bill Clinton and Hillary Clinton.

§ **Ralph Nader (1934)** - Consumer advocate, lawyer, and political activist known for his work on consumer protection.

February 28th

v **Bernadette Peters (1948)** - Actress, singer, and Broadway performer known for her roles in musicals like "Into the Woods" and "Annie Get Your Gun."

v **Jason Aldean (1977)** - Country music singer known for hits like "Dirt Road Anthem" and "My Kinda Party."

v **Gilbert Gottfried (1955)** - Comedian and voice actor known for his distinctive voice and roles in animation.

v **Ali Larter (1976)** - Actress recognized for her roles in films like "Final Destination" and the TV series "Heroes."

v **Rae Dawn Chong (1961)** - Actress known for her roles in "The Color Purple" and "Commando."

February 29th

Ø **Ja Rule (1976)** - Rapper, singer, and actor known for his contributions to the hip-hop genre.

Ø **Antonio Sabàto Jr. (1972)** - Italian-American actor and model known for his roles in TV series like "General Hospital" and "Melrose Place."

Ø **Dennis Farina (1944)** - Actor and former police officer recognized for his roles in "Get Shorty" and "Law & Order."

Ø **Gioachino Rossini (1792)** - Italian composer known for his operas, including "The Barber of Seville" and "William Tell."

Ø **Michelle Yeoh (1962)** - Malaysian actress and producer known for her roles in "Crouching Tiger, Hidden Dragon" and "Tomorrow Never Dies."

March Birthdays

March 1st

·   **Frederic Chopin (1810)** - Polish composer and virtuoso pianist known for his romantic era compositions.

·   **Justin Bieber (1994)** - Canadian singer-songwriter who gained fame at a young age and has become a pop sensation.

·   **Ron Howard (1954)** - Actor, filmmaker, and director known for directing films like "A Beautiful Mind" and "Apollo 13."

·   **Lupita Nyong'o (1983)** - Kenyan-Mexican actress and Academy Award winner for her role in "12 Years a Slave."

·   **Jensen Ackles (1978)** - Actor known for his role as Dean Winchester on the TV series "Supernatural."

March 2nd

o **Dr. Seuss (1904)** - American author and illustrator known for children's classics like "The Cat in the Hat" and "Green Eggs and Ham."

o **Jon Bon Jovi (1962)** - Singer-songwriter and frontman of the rock band Bon Jovi.

o **Daniel Craig (1968)** - British actor known for his role as James Bond in the modern film series.

o **Rebel Wilson (1980)** - Australian actress and comedian known for her roles in "Pitch Perfect" and "Bridesmaids."

o **Bryce Dallas Howard (1981)** - Actress recognized for her roles in "Jurassic World" and "The Help."

March 3rd

§ **Alexander Graham Bell (1847)** - Inventor credited with developing the first practical telephone.

§ **Jessica Biel (1982)** - Actress known for her roles in "7th Heaven" and films like "The Illusionist" and "Total Recall."

§ **Hattie McDaniel (1895)** - Actress and singer, the first African American to win an Academy Award for her role in "Gone with the Wind."

§ **Julie Bowen (1970)** - Actress known for her role in the TV series "Modern Family" and "Boston Legal."

§ **Miranda Richardson (1958)** - British actress known for her roles in "The Crying Game" and "Harry Potter" films.

March 4th

v **Patricia Heaton (1958)** - Actress recognized for her roles in TV series like "Everybody Loves Raymond" and "The Middle."

v **Chaz Bono (1969)** - Activist, author, and musician who became prominent for his transgender advocacy.

v **Brooklyn Beckham (1999)** - British model and photographer, son of David and Victoria Beckham.

v **Paula Prentiss (1938)** - Actress known for her roles in films like "The Stepford Wives" and "Catch-22."

v **Catherine O'Hara (1954)** - Canadian actress and comedian known for her roles in "Home Alone" and "Schitt's Creek."

March 5th

Ø **Joel Osteen (1963)** - Televangelist, author, and pastor of Lakewood Church in Houston, Texas.

Ø **Eva Mendes (1974)** - Actress known for her roles in films like "Hitch" and "Training Day."

Ø **Rex Harrison (1908)** - British actor known for his role as Professor Henry Higgins in "My Fair Lady."

Ø **Penn Jillette (1955)** - Magician, illusionist, and one-half of the magic duo "Penn & Teller."

Ø **Matt Lucas (1974)** - British comedian and actor known for his roles in the TV series "Little Britain" and "Doctor Who."

March 6th

ü **Michelangelo (1475)** - Renowned Italian Renaissance sculptor, painter, architect, and poet.

ü **Rob Reiner (1947)** - Filmmaker and actor known for directing films like "When Harry Met Sally..." and "The Princess Bride."

ü **Shaquille O'Neal (1972)** - Former NBA basketball player and sports analyst, known for his dominant presence on the court.

ü **Connie Britton (1967)** - Actress known for her roles in TV series like "Friday Night Lights" and "Nashville."

ü **Ellen Muth (1981)** - Actress recognized for her role in the TV series "Dead Like Me."

March 7th

·   **Rachel Weisz (1970)** - British actress known for her roles in "The Mummy," "The Constant Gardener," and "The Favourite."

·   **Bryan Cranston (1956)** - Actor known for his iconic role as Walter White in the TV series "Breaking Bad."

·   **Wanda Sykes (1964)** - Comedian, actress, and writer known for her stand-up comedy and roles in TV shows and films.

·   **Peter Sarsgaard (1971)** - Actor known for his roles in films like "Boys Don't Cry" and "Shattered Glass."

·   **Maurice Ravel (1875)** - French composer known for his impressionist music and compositions like "Boléro."

March 8th

§ **Freddie Prinze Jr. (1976)** - Actor known for his roles in "She's All That" and "Scooby-Doo."

§ **James Van Der Beek (1977)** - Actor recognized for his role in the TV series "Dawson's Creek."

§ **Micky Dolenz (1945)** - Musician and actor, best known as the drummer and vocalist of The Monkees.

§ **Aidan Quinn (1959)** - Actor known for his roles in films like "Legends of the Fall" and "Benny & Joon."

§ **Kat Von D (1982)** - Tattoo artist, entrepreneur, and TV personality known for the show "LA Ink."

March 9th

v **Brittany Snow (1986)** - Actress known for her roles in "Pitch Perfect," "Hairspray," and TV series like "American Dreams."

v **Oscar Isaac (1979)** - Actor known for his roles in "Inside Llewyn Davis," "Star Wars," and "Ex Machina."

v **Bobby Fischer (1943)** - Chess prodigy and grandmaster, considered one of the greatest chess players of all time.

v **Juliette Binoche (1964)** - French actress known for her roles in "The English Patient" and "Chocolat."

v **Bow Wow (1987)** - Rapper and actor who gained fame as a child artist and continued in the entertainment industry.

March 10th

Ø **Chuck Norris (1940)** - Martial artist, actor, and cultural icon known for his roles in action films and TV series like "Walker, Texas Ranger."

Ø **Sharon Stone (1958)** - Actress known for her roles in "Basic Instinct," "Casino," and "Total Recall."

Ø **Olivia Wilde (1984)** - Actress known for her roles in TV series like "House" and films like "Tron: Legacy" and "Booksmart."

Ø **Jon Hamm (1971)** - Actor recognized for his role as Don Draper in the TV series "Mad Men."

Ø **Emily Osment (1992)** - Actress and singer known for her role in the TV series "Hannah Montana."

March 11th

ü **Anton Yelchin (1989)** - Actor known for his roles in "Star Trek" films and "Charlie Bartlett."

ü **Johnny Knoxville (1971)** - Actor and comedian known for creating and starring in "Jackass" series.

ü **Thora Birch (1982)** - Actress recognized for roles in "American Beauty" and "Ghost World."

ü **Terrence Howard (1969)** - Actor known for his roles in "Hustle & Flow" and "Empire."

ü **Rupert Murdoch (1931)** - Media mogul and founder of News Corporation.

March 12th

· **Liza Minnelli (1946)** - Actress and singer known for her roles in musical films like "Cabaret."

· **Mitt Romney (1947)** - Politician and businessman, former Governor of Massachusetts.

· **Aaron Eckhart (1968)** - Actor recognized for roles in "The Dark Knight" and "Thank You for Smoking."

· **Darryl Strawberry (1962)** - Former MLB player and baseball legend.

· **James Taylor (1948)** - Singer-songwriter known for folk and rock hits like "Fire and Rain."

March 13th

o **William H. Macy (1950)** - Actor known for roles in "Fargo" and "Shameless."

o **Adam Clayton (1960)** - Bassist of the rock band U2.

o **Common (1972)** - Rapper and actor known for his socially conscious music and acting.

o **Emile Hirsch (1985)** - Actor recognized for roles in "Into the Wild" and "Speed Racer."

o **Kaya Scodelario (1992)** - British actress known for her role in "Skins" and "The Maze Runner."

March 14th

§ **Albert Einstein (1879)** - Theoretical physicist, known for his theory of relativity.

§ **Billy Crystal (1948)** - Comedian and actor known for roles in films like "When Harry Met Sally..." and hosting the Oscars.

§ **Michael Caine (1933)** - British actor known for roles in "The Dark Knight" trilogy and "The Cider House Rules."

§ **Ansel Elgort (1994)** - Actor known for "The Fault in Our Stars" and "Baby Driver."

§ **Quincy Jones (1933)** - Music producer, composer, and influential figure in the music industry.

March 15th

v **Eva Longoria (1975)** - Actress known for her role in TV series "Desperate Housewives."

v **Ruth Bader Ginsburg (1933)** - Former U.S. Supreme Court Justice and women's rights advocate.

v **Kellan Lutz (1985)** - Actor recognized for his role as Emmett Cullen in "Twilight" series.

v **Andrew Jackson (1767)** - 7th President of the United States.

v **will.i.am (1975)** - Rapper, singer, and member of the Black Eyed Peas.

March 16th

Ø **Jerry Lewis (1926)** - Comedian, actor, and filmmaker known for slapstick comedy.

Ø **Flavor Flav (1959)** - Rapper and member of the hip-hop group Public Enemy.

Ø **Alexandra Daddario (1986)** - Actress recognized for roles in "Percy Jackson" films and "Baywatch."

Ø **Blake Griffin (1989)** - NBA basketball player known for his powerful dunks.

Ø **Victor Garber (1949)** - Actor known for roles in TV shows like "Alias" and "Legends of Tomorrow."

March 17th

ü **Rob Lowe (1964)** - Actor known for roles in "Parks and Recreation" and "The West Wing."

ü **Nat King Cole (1919)** - Legendary jazz singer and pianist.

ü **Mia Hamm (1972)** - Former professional soccer player and two-time Olympic gold medalist.

ü **Kurt Russell (1951)** - Actor known for roles in "Escape from New York" and "The Hateful Eight."

ü **John Boyega (1992)** - British actor recognized for his role in "Star Wars: The Force Awakens."

March 18th

· **Adam Levine (1979)** - Singer-songwriter and lead vocalist of Maroon 5.

· **Queen Latifah (1970)** - Rapper, actress, and singer known for her versatile career.

· **Dane Cook (1972)** - Comedian and actor recognized for stand-up comedy and films like "Good Luck Chuck."

· **Vanessa Williams (1963)** - Actress, singer, and former Miss America.

· **Lily Collins (1989)** - Actress known for roles in "The Mortal Instruments" and "Emily in Paris."

March 19th

○ **Bruce Willis (1955)** - Actor known for roles in "Die Hard" series and "The Sixth Sense."

○ **Glenn Close (1947)** - Actress known for roles in "Fatal Attraction" and "The Wife."

○ **Garrett Clayton (1991)** - Actor recognized for his role in Disney Channel's "Teen Beach Movie."

○ **Ursula Andress (1936)** - Swiss actress known for her iconic role as Bond girl Honey Ryder.

○ **Rachel Blanchard (1976)** - Canadian actress known for her roles in TV series like "Clueless" and "You Me Her."

March 20th

§ **Spike Lee (1957)** - Filmmaker known for directing films like "Do the Right Thing" and "Malcolm X."

§ **William Hurt (1950)** - Actor recognized for roles in "Kiss of the Spider Woman" and "A History of Violence."

§ **Holly Hunter (1958)** - Actress known for her roles in "The Piano" and "Broadcast News."

§ **Fred Rogers (1928)** - Television host of "Mister Rogers' Neighborhood."

§ **Bianca Lawson (1979)** - Actress recognized for her roles in TV series like "Pretty Little Liars" and "Teen Wolf."

March 21st

v **Rosie O'Donnell (1962)** - Comedian, actress, and TV host.

v **Matthew Broderick (1962)** - Actor known for roles in "Ferris Bueller's Day Off" and "The Producers."

v **Scott Eastwood (1986)** - Actor recognized for roles in "Suicide Squad" and "The Fate of the Furious."

v **Gary Oldman (1958)** - British actor known for roles in "The Dark Knight" trilogy and "Darkest Hour."

v **Timothy Dalton (1946)** - Actor recognized for portraying James Bond.

March 22nd

Ø **William Shatner (1931)** - Actor known for his role as Captain Kirk in "Star Trek."

Ø **Reese Witherspoon (1976)** - Actress known for roles in "Legally Blonde" and "Walk the Line."

Ø **Andrew Lloyd Webber (1948)** - British composer and musical theater legend.

Ø **Keegan-Michael Key (1971)** - Comedian and actor known for "Key & Peele" and "The Prom."

Ø **Stephanie Mills (1957)** - R&B and Broadway singer known for her powerful vocals.

March 23rd

ü **Keri Russell (1976)** - Actress known for roles in TV series "Felicity" and "The Americans."

ü **Perez Hilton (1978)** - Celebrity blogger and media personality.

ü **Jason Dohring (1982)** - Actor recognized for his role as Logan in TV series "Veronica Mars."

ü **Joan Crawford (1905)** - Legendary actress known for her roles in classic films.

ü **Kyrie Irving (1992)** - NBA basketball player known for his skills on the court.

March 24th

· **Keisha Castle-Hughes (1990)** - New Zealand actress known for roles in "Whale Rider" and "Game of Thrones."

· **Jessica Chastain (1977)** - Actress known for roles in "Zero Dark Thirty" and "Interstellar."

· **Lake Bell (1979)** - Actress, director, and screenwriter known for "In a World..." and "Childrens Hospital."

· **Harry Houdini (1874)** - Illusionist and escape artist.

· **Alyson Hannigan (1974)** - Actress recognized for roles in TV series "Buffy the Vampire Slayer" and "How I Met Your Mother."

March 25th

o **Elton John (1947)** - British singer-songwriter and pop music legend.

o **Sarah Jessica Parker (1965)** - Actress known for her role as Carrie Bradshaw in "Sex and the City."

o **Marcia Cross (1962)** - Actress recognized for her role in TV series "Desperate Housewives."

o **Danica Patrick (1982)** - Former professional racing driver.

o **Katharine McPhee (1984)** - Singer and actress known for "American Idol" and "Smash."

March 26th

§ **Keira Knightley (1985)** - British actress known for roles in "Pirates of the Caribbean" and "Pride & Prejudice."

§ **Diana Ross (1944)** - Legendary singer and former member of The Supremes.

§ **Jennifer Grey (1960)** - Actress known for her role in "Dirty Dancing."

§ **Leslie Mann (1972)** - Actress recognized for roles in "Knocked Up" and "The 40-Year-Old Virgin."

§ **James Caan (1940)** - Actor known for roles in "The Godfather" and "Misery."

March 27th

v **Mariah Carey (1969)** - Singer-songwriter known for her multi-octave vocal range and hit songs.

v **Fergie (1975)** - Singer known for her work with The Black Eyed Peas and solo career.

v **Quentin Tarantino (1963)** - Filmmaker known for directing films like "Pulp Fiction" and "Kill Bill."

v **Jessie J (1988)** - British singer-songwriter known for hits like "Price Tag" and "Bang Bang."

v **Pauley Perrette (1969)** - Actress recognized for her role in TV series "NCIS."

March 28th

Ø **Lady Gaga (1986)** - Singer, songwriter, and actress known for her theatrical style and music.

Ø **Vince Vaughn (1970)** - Actor known for roles in "Wedding Crashers" and "Swingers."

Ø **Reba McEntire (1955)** - Country music singer and actress.

Ø **Julia Stiles (1981)** - Actress recognized for roles in "10 Things I Hate About You" and "Save the Last Dance."

Ø **Dianne Wiest (1948)** - Actress known for her roles in films directed by Woody Allen.

March 29th

ü **Lucy Lawless (1968)** - Actress known for her role as Xena in TV series "Xena: Warrior Princess."

ü **Eric Idle (1943)** - British comedian, actor, and member of Monty Python.

ü **Elle Macpherson (1964)** - Australian model and actress known as "The Body."

ü **Brendan Gleeson (1955)** - Irish actor recognized for roles in "In Bruges" and "Harry Potter" series.

ü **Terence Hill (1939)** - Italian actor known for spaghetti western films.

March 30th

- **Eric Clapton (1945)** - British rock guitarist and singer-songwriter.

- **Celine Dion (1968)** - Canadian singer known for her powerful vocals and hit songs.

- **Robbie Coltrane (1950)** - Scottish actor recognized for his role as Hagrid in "Harry Potter" series.

- **Norah Jones (1979)** - Singer-songwriter known for her soulful jazz and folk music.

- **Tracy Chapman (1964)** - Singer-songwriter known for her hits like "Fast Car" and "Talkin' 'bout a Revolution."

March 31st

o **Ewan McGregor (1971)** - Scottish actor known for his roles in "Trainspotting" and the "Star Wars" prequel trilogy.

o **Shirley Jones (1934)** - Actress and singer recognized for her roles in "The Partridge Family" and "Oklahoma!"

- **Christopher Walken (1943)** - Actor known for his unique voice and roles in "The Deer Hunter" and "Pulp Fiction."

- **Rhea Perlman (1948)** - Actress recognized for her role as Carla on TV series "Cheers."

- **Al Gore (1948)** - Former Vice President of the United States and environmental activist.

April Birthdays

April 1st

· **Susan Boyle (1961)** - Scottish singer known for her appearance on "Britain's Got Talent."

· **Rachel Maddow (1973)** - Television host, political commentator, and host of "The Rachel Maddow Show."

· **Asa Butterfield (1997)** - British actor recognized for his roles in "Hugo" and "Ender's Game."

· **Taran Killam (1982)** - Actor and comedian known for his work on "Saturday Night Live."

· **Ali MacGraw (1939)** - Actress known for her roles in "Love Story" and "The Getaway."

April 2nd

o **Emmylou Harris (1947)** - Singer-songwriter known for her contributions to country and folk music.

o **Christopher Meloni (1961)** - Actor recognized for his roles in "Law & Order: SVU" and "Oz."

o **Michael Fassbender (1977)** - Actor known for his roles in "Inglourious Basterds" and the "X-Men" series.

o **Clark Gregg (1962)** - Actor known for his role as Agent Coulson in the Marvel Cinematic Universe.

o **Linda Hunt (1945)** - Actress known for her role in "The Year of Living Dangerously."

April 3rd

§ **Alec Baldwin (1958)** - Actor known for his roles in "30 Rock" and "The Departed."

§ **Eddie Murphy (1961)** - Comedian and actor known for his work on "Saturday Night Live" and films like "Coming to America."

§ **Amanda Bynes (1986)** - Actress known for her roles in TV series like "The Amanda Show" and "What I Like About You."

§ **Marlon Brando (1924)** - Legendary actor known for roles in "The Godfather" and "A Streetcar Named Desire."

§ **Jane Goodall (1934)** - British primatologist and anthropologist known for her groundbreaking work with chimpanzees.

April 4th

v **Robert Downey Jr. (1965)** - Actor known for his portrayal of Tony Stark/Iron Man in the Marvel Cinematic Universe.

v **Heath Ledger (1979)** - Australian actor known for his roles in "Brokeback Mountain" and "The Dark Knight."

v **David Cross (1964)** - Comedian and actor known for his role in "Arrested Development."

v **Sarah Gadon (1987)** - Canadian actress recognized for her roles in "Cosmopolis" and "Alias Grace."

v **Maya Angelou (1928)** - Poet, memoirist, and civil rights activist known for her powerful writing.

April 5th

Pharrell Williams (1973) - Music producer, singer, and member of the music duo The Neptunes.

Hayley Atwell (1982) - British-American actress known for her role as Peggy Carter in the Marvel Cinematic Universe.

Agnetha Fältskog (1950) - Swedish singer known as a member of the iconic pop group ABBA.

Sterling K. Brown (1976) - Actor recognized for his roles in "This Is Us" and "Black Panther."

Bette Davis (1908) - Acclaimed actress known for her roles in classic films like "All About Eve."

April 6th

· **Paul Rudd (1969)** - Actor known for his roles in "Ant-Man" and "Anchorman."

· **Candace Cameron Bure (1976)** - Actress recognized for her role as D.J. Tanner on "Full House."

· **Zach Braff (1975)** - Actor known for his role in TV series "Scrubs" and film "Garden State."

· **John Ratzenberger (1947)** - Actor known for his role as Cliff Clavin on TV series "Cheers."

· **Merle Haggard (1937)** - Country music legend known for hits like "Okie from Muskogee."

April 7th

· **Russell Crowe (1964)** - Actor known for his roles in "Gladiator" and "A Beautiful Mind."

· **Jackie Chan (1954)** - Hong Kong actor, martial artist, and filmmaker known for action-comedy films.

· **Billie Holiday (1915)** - Legendary jazz singer known for her emotional and distinctive voice.

· **James Garner (1928)** - Actor recognized for his roles in TV series "Maverick" and "The Rockford Files."

· **Francis Ford Coppola (1939)** - Film director known for classics like "The Godfather" trilogy and "Apocalypse Now."

April 8th

o **Patricia Arquette (1968)** - Actress known for roles in "Boyhood" and "Medium."

o **Robin Wright (1966)** - Actress recognized for her role in TV series "House of Cards."

o **Taylor Kitsch (1981)** - Actor known for roles in "Friday Night Lights" and "X-Men Origins: Wolverine."

o **Julian Lennon (1963)** - Musician and singer-songwriter, son of John Lennon.

o **Biz Markie (1964)** - Rapper, beatboxer, and DJ known for his hit single "Just a Friend."

April 9th

§ **Kristen Stewart (1990)** - Actress known for her role as Bella Swan in the "Twilight" series.

§ **Cynthia Nixon (1966)** - Actress recognized for her role as Miranda Hobbes in TV series "Sex and the City."

§ **Dennis Quaid (1954)** - Actor known for roles in films like "The Right Stuff" and "The Parent Trap."

§ **Leighton Meester (1986)** - Actress and singer recognized for her role as Blair Waldorf in "Gossip Girl."

§ **Hugh Hefner (1926)** - Founder of Playboy magazine and cultural icon.

April 10th

v **Steven Seagal (1952)** - Actor and martial artist known for action films like "Under Siege."

v **Mandy Moore (1984)** - Actress and singer recognized for her roles in "A Walk to Remember" and "This Is Us."

v **David Harbour (1975)** - Actor known for his role as Chief Jim Hopper in "Stranger Things."

v **Charlie Hunnam (1980)** - British actor recognized for his role in TV series "Sons of Anarchy."

v **Daisy Ridley (1992)** - British actress known for her role as Rey in the "Star Wars" sequel trilogy.

April 11th

Ø **Joss Stone (1987)** - British singer-songwriter known for her soulful voice and hits like "Super Duper Love."

Ø **Alessandra Ambrosio (1981)** - Brazilian model and Victoria's Secret Angel.

Ø **Dakota Blue Richards (1994)** - British actress recognized for her role in the film "The Golden Compass."

Ø **Jennifer Esposito (1973)** - Actress known for her roles in TV series "Blue Bloods" and "NCIS."

Ø **Vincent Gallo (1961)** - Actor, director, and musician known for his versatile career.

April 12th

ü **David Letterman (1947)** - Comedian and television host known for "Late Night with David Letterman" and "The Late Show."

ü **Saoirse Ronan (1994)** - Irish-American actress recognized for her roles in "Lady Bird" and "Brooklyn."

ü **Claire Danes (1979)** - Actress known for her roles in TV series "Homeland" and "My So-Called Life."

ü **Shannen Doherty (1971)** - Actress recognized for her roles in TV series "Beverly Hills, 90210" and "Charmed."

ü **Andy Garcia (1956)** - Actor known for his roles in "The Godfather Part III" and "Ocean's Eleven."

April 13th

·   **Thomas Jefferson (1743)** - Third President of the United States and principal author of the Declaration of Independence.

·   **Ron Perlman (1950)** - Actor known for his roles in "Hellboy" and TV series "Sons of Anarchy."

·   **Al Green (1946)** - Singer known for his soul and gospel music, including hits like "Let's Stay Together."

·   **Ricky Schroder (1970)** - Actor recognized for his roles in TV series "Silver Spoons" and "NYPD Blue."

·   **Allison Williams (1988)** - Actress recognized for her role in TV series "Girls."

April 14th

o **Sarah Michelle Gellar (1977)** - Actress known for her role as Buffy in TV series "Buffy the Vampire Slayer."

o **Abigail Breslin (1996)** - Actress recognized for her roles in films like "Little Miss Sunshine" and "Zombieland."

o **Pete Rose (1941)** - Former MLB player and all-time hits leader.

o **Brad Garrett (1960)** - Actor known for his role in TV series "Everybody Loves Raymond."

o **Robert Carlyle (1961)** - Scottish actor recognized for his roles in "Trainspotting" and "Once Upon a Time."

April 15th

§ **Emma Watson (1990)** - British actress known for her role as Hermione Granger in the "Harry Potter" series.

§ **Maisie Williams (1997)** - British actress recognized for her role as Arya Stark in "Game of Thrones."

§ **Seth Rogen (1982)** - Actor and comedian known for roles in "Knocked Up" and "Superbad."

§ **Leonardo da Vinci (1452)** - Italian polymath known for his contributions to art, science, and inventions.

§ **Emma Thompson (1959)** - British actress known for her roles in "Sense and Sensibility" and "Nanny McPhee."

April 16th

v **Charlie Chaplin (1889)** - Iconic actor, filmmaker, and silent film star known for his character "The Tramp."

v **Chance the Rapper (1993)** - Rapper, singer, and songwriter known for his innovative hip-hop music.

v **Martin Lawrence (1965)** - Comedian and actor known for his roles in "Bad Boys" and TV series "Martin."

v **Ellen Barkin (1954)** - Actress recognized for her roles in "The Big Easy" and "Sea of Love."

v **Gina Carano (1982)** - Former mixed martial artist and actress known for her role in "The Mandalorian."

April 17th

Ø **Jennifer Garner (1972)** - Actress known for her roles in TV series "Alias" and films like "13 Going on 30."

Ø **Sean Bean (1959)** - British actor recognized for roles in "The Lord of the Rings" and "Game of Thrones."

Ø **Victoria Beckham (1974)** - Singer, fashion designer, and member of the Spice Girls.

Ø **Rooney Mara (1985)** - Actress known for her roles in "The Girl with the Dragon Tattoo" and "Carol."

Ø **Maynard James Keenan (1964)** - Musician and frontman of rock bands Tool and A Perfect Circle.

April 18th

ü **Melissa Joan Hart (1976)** - Actress recognized for her roles in TV series "Sabrina the Teenage Witch" and "Clarissa Explains It All."

ü **Kourtney Kardashian (1979)** - Television personality and member of the Kardashian-Jenner family.

ü **America Ferrera (1984)** - Actress known for her role in TV series "Ugly Betty" and "Superstore."

ü **James Woods (1947)** - Actor known for roles in "Once Upon a Time in America" and "Casino."

ü **Conan O'Brien (1963)** - Comedian and television host known for "Late Night with Conan O'Brien" and "Conan."

April 19th

·   **Kate Hudson (1979)** - Actress known for her roles in "Almost Famous" and "How to Lose a Guy in 10 Days."

·   **Hayden Christensen (1981)** - Actor recognized for his role as Anakin Skywalker in "Star Wars" prequel trilogy.

·   **Maria Sharapova (1987)** - Former professional tennis player and five-time Grand Slam champion.

·   **Tim Curry (1946)** - British actor known for roles in "The Rocky Horror Picture Show" and "It."

·   **Ashley Judd (1968)** - Actress recognized for her roles in "Double Jeopardy" and "Divergent."

April 20th

o **Jessica Lange (1949)** - Actress known for her roles in "Tootsie" and "American Horror Story."

o **Miranda Kerr (1983)** - Australian model and Victoria's Secret Angel.

o **Carmen Electra (1972)** - Actress and model known for her appearances in "Baywatch" and Playboy.

o **Andy Serkis (1964)** - British actor recognized for his motion capture roles in "The Lord of the Rings" and "Planet of the Apes" series.

o **Joey Lawrence (1976)** - Actor and singer recognized for his roles in TV series "Blossom" and "Melissa & Joey."

April 21st

§ **Queen Elizabeth II (1926)** - Current reigning monarch of the United Kingdom.

§ **James McAvoy (1979)** - Scottish actor known for roles in "X-Men" series and "Split."

§ **Tony Romo (1980)** - Former NFL quarterback and current sports commentator.

§ **Andie MacDowell (1958)** - Actress recognized for her roles in "Groundhog Day" and "Four Weddings and a Funeral."

§ **Iggy Pop (1947)** - Rock musician known for his influential career as the "Godfather of Punk."

April 22nd

v **Jack Nicholson (1937)** - Legendary actor known for roles in "One Flew Over the Cuckoo's Nest" and "The Shining."

v **Amber Heard (1986)** - Actress known for her roles in "Aquaman" and "Pineapple Express."

v **Machine Gun Kelly (1990)** - Rapper, singer, and actor.

v **Jeffrey Dean Morgan (1966)** - Actor recognized for his roles in TV series "The Walking Dead" and "Grey's Anatomy."

v **Marshawn Lynch (1986)** - Former NFL running back known for his powerful playing style.

April 23rd

Ø **John Cena (1977)** - Professional wrestler, actor, and television host.

Ø **Gigi Hadid (1995)** - American model known for her appearances in major fashion campaigns.

Ø **George Lopez (1961)** - Comedian and actor known for his sitcom "George Lopez" and stand-up comedy.

Ø **Jaime King (1979)** - Actress recognized for her roles in "Sin City" and TV series "Hart of Dixie."

Ø **Valerie Bertinelli (1960)** - Actress known for her roles in TV series "One Day at a Time" and "Hot in Cleveland."

April 24th

ü **Kelly Clarkson (1982)** - Singer-songwriter and winner of the first season of "American Idol."

ü **Barbra Streisand (1942)** - Iconic singer, actress, and filmmaker.

ü **Sachin Tendulkar (1973)** - Former Indian cricketer, widely regarded as one of the greatest batsmen in cricket history.

ü **Cedric the Entertainer (1964)** - Comedian, actor, and host known for "The Original Kings of Comedy" and "The Steve Harvey Show."

ü **Jack Quaid (1992)** - Actor recognized for his roles in "The Hunger Games" and TV series "The Boys."

April 25th

·   **Al Pacino (1940)** - Legendary actor known for roles in "The Godfather" series and "Scarface."

·   **Renee Zellweger (1969)** - Actress known for her roles in "Bridget Jones's Diary" and "Chicago."

·   **Ella Fitzgerald (1917)** - Legendary jazz singer known as the "First Lady of Song."

·   **Sara Paxton (1988)** - Actress recognized for her roles in "Aquamarine" and "The Innkeepers."

·   **Jason Lee (1970)** - Actor and former professional skateboarder known for his role in TV series "My Name Is Earl."

April 26th

o **Channing Tatum (1980)** - Actor known for his roles in "Magic Mike" and "21 Jump Street."

o **Melania Trump (1970)** - Former First Lady of the United States.

o **Kevin James (1965)** - Comedian and actor known for his role in TV series "The King of Queens."

o **Carol Burnett (1933)** - Actress, comedian, and television host known for "The Carol Burnett Show."

o **Jet Li (1963)** - Chinese actor and martial artist known for action films like "Lethal Weapon 4" and "Hero."

April 27th

§ **Jenna Coleman (1986)** - British actress recognized for her role as Clara Oswald in "Doctor Who."

§ **Sheena Easton (1959)** - Scottish singer known for hits like "Morning Train" and "For Your Eyes Only."

§ **Ari Graynor (1983)** - Actress recognized for her roles in "Nick & Norah's Infinite Playlist" and "The Sopranos."

§ **Sally Hawkins (1976)** - Actress known for her roles in "The Shape of Water" and "Blue Jasmine."

§ **Cory Booker (1969)** - U.S. Senator and former Mayor of Newark, New Jersey.

April 28th

v **Penélope Cruz (1974)** - Spanish actress known for her roles in "Vicky Cristina Barcelona" and "Pirates of the Caribbean."

v **Jessica Alba (1981)** - Actress and businesswoman recognized for roles in "Sin City" and "Fantastic Four."

v **Jorge Garcia (1973)** - Actor known for his role in TV series "Lost."

v **Ann-Margret (1941)** - Actress and singer recognized for her roles in "Viva Las Vegas" and "Carnal Knowledge."

v **Jay Leno (1950)** - Comedian and television host known for hosting "The Tonight Show with Jay Leno."

April 29th

Ø **Michelle Pfeiffer (1958)** - Actress known for her roles in "Scarface" and "Batman Returns."

Ø **Daniel Day-Lewis (1957)** - Acclaimed actor known for roles in "There Will Be Blood" and "Lincoln."

Ø **Master P (1970)** - Rapper, actor, and entrepreneur known for his contributions to hip-hop.

Ø **Uma Thurman (1970)** - Actress recognized for her roles in "Pulp Fiction" and "Kill Bill" series.

Ø **Jerry Seinfeld (1954)** - Comedian and actor known for his eponymous sitcom "Seinfeld."

April 30th

ü **Gal Gadot (1985)** - Israeli actress known for her role as Wonder Woman in the DC Extended Universe.

ü **Kirsten Dunst (1982)** - Actress recognized for her roles in "Spider-Man" and "Interview with the Vampire."

ü **Queen Carl XVI Gustaf of Sweden (1946)** - King of Sweden since 1973.

ü **Isiah Thomas (1961)** - Former NBA player and Hall of Famer.

ü **Johnny Galecki (1975)** - Actor known for his role as Leonard Hofstadter in TV series "The Big Bang Theory."

May Birthdays

May 1st

·   **Jamie Dornan (1982)** - Northern Irish actor known for his role in the "Fifty Shades" film series.

·   **Tim McGraw (1967)** - Country music singer and actor.

·   **Wes Anderson (1969)** - Filmmaker known for his distinctive visual style and films like "The Grand Budapest Hotel."

·   **Judy Collins (1939)** - Folk singer known for hits like "Both Sides, Now."

·   **D'Arcy Carden (1980)** - Actress recognized for her role in TV series "The Good Place."

May 2nd

o **Dwayne "The Rock" Johnson (1972)** - Actor, former professional wrestler, and producer.

o **David Beckham (1975)** - Former professional footballer and fashion icon.

o **Ellie Kemper (1980)** - Actress known for her role in TV series "The Office" and "Unbreakable Kimmy Schmidt."

o **Lily Allen (1985)** - British singer-songwriter known for hits like "Smile" and "The Fear."

o **Donatella Versace (1955)** - Italian fashion designer and Vice President of Versace Group.

May 3rd

§ **Bing Crosby (1903)** - Legendary singer and actor known for classics like "White Christmas."

§ **Christina Hendricks (1975)** - Actress recognized for her role in TV series "Mad Men."

§ **James Brown (1933)** - "Godfather of Soul" and influential singer and performer.

§ **Frankie Valli (1934)** - Lead singer of the band The Four Seasons.

§ **Cheryl Burke (1984)** - Professional dancer known for her appearances on "Dancing with the Stars."

May 4th

v **Audrey Hepburn (1929)** - Iconic actress known for roles in "Breakfast at Tiffany's" and "Roman Holiday."

v **Will Arnett (1970)** - Actor known for his roles in "Arrested Development" and voicing Lego Batman.

v **Rory McIlroy (1989)** - Professional golfer from Northern Ireland.

v **Cesc Fàbregas (1987)** - Spanish professional footballer.

v **Lance Bass (1979)** - Singer and member of the boy band NSYNC.

May 5th

Ø **Adele (1988)** - British singer-songwriter known for her powerful vocals and hit songs.

Ø **Henry Cavill (1983)** - British actor known for his role as Superman in the DC Extended Universe.

Ø **Karl Marx (1818)** - Philosopher, economist, and author of "The Communist Manifesto."

Ø **Chris Brown (1989)** - Singer, songwriter, and actor.

Ø **Michael Palin (1943)** - British comedian, actor, and member of Monty Python.

May 6th

ü **George Clooney (1961)** - Actor, filmmaker, and philanthropist known for his roles in "Ocean's Eleven" and "Gravity."

ü **Gabourey Sidibe (1983)** - Actress known for her role in the film "Precious."

ü **Sigmund Freud (1856)** - Austrian neurologist and founder of psychoanalysis.

ü **Tony Blair (1953)** - Former Prime Minister of the United Kingdom.

ü **Adrianne Palicki (1983)** - Actress recognized for her roles in TV series "Friday Night Lights" and "Agents of S.H.I.E.L.D."

May 7th

· **Breckin Meyer (1974)** - Actor known for his roles in "Clueless" and "Road Trip."

· **Robert Browning (1812)** - English poet and playwright.

· **Alexander Ludwig (1992)** - Canadian actor recognized for his roles in "The Hunger Games" and "Vikings."

· **Traci Lords (1968) -** Actress and singer known for her appearances in adult films and mainstream media.

· **Johannes Brahms (1833)** - Renowned German composer and pianist.

May 8th

o **Enrique Iglesias (1975)** - Spanish singer-songwriter known for his Latin pop music.

o **Melissa Gilbert (1964)** - Actress recognized for her role as Laura Ingalls Wilder on TV series "Little House on the Prairie."

o **David Attenborough (1926)** - British broadcaster and natural historian known for his documentaries.

o **Stephen Amell (1981)** - Canadian actor known for his role in TV series "Arrow."

o **Don Rickles (1926)** - Comedian and actor known for his sharp wit and insult comedy.

May 9th

§ **Billy Joel (1949)** - Singer-songwriter and pianist known for hits like "Piano Man" and "Uptown Girl."

§ **Rosario Dawson (1979)** - Actress recognized for her roles in films like "Sin City" and "Rent."

§ **Albert Finney (1936)** - British actor known for roles in "Tom Jones" and "Erin Brockovich."

§ **Candice Bergen (1946)** - Actress known for her role in TV series "Murphy Brown."

§ **Prince Fielder (1984)** - Former MLB first baseman and designated hitter.

May 10th

v **Bono (1960)** - Lead vocalist of the rock band U2 and philanthropist.

v **Kenan Thompson (1978)** - Actor and comedian known for his work on "Saturday Night Live."

v **Bono (1960)** - Lead vocalist of the rock band U2 and philanthropist.

v **Kenan Thompson (1978)** - Actor and comedian known for his work on "Saturday Night Live."

v **Lindsey Shaw (1989)** - Actress recognized for her role in TV series "Ned's Declassified School Survival Guide."

May 11th

Ø **Salvador Dalí (1904)** - Spanish surrealist artist known for his distinctive and imaginative paintings.

Ø **Cory Monteith (1982)** - Canadian actor recognized for his role in TV series "Glee."

Ø **Martha Quinn (1959)** - Former MTV VJ and television host.

Ø **Cam Newton (1989)** - NFL quarterback and former MVP.

Ø **Natasha Richardson (1963)** - British actress known for her roles in films like "The Parent Trap."

May 12th

ü **Florence Nightingale (1820)** - English social reformer and founder of modern nursing.

ü **Tony Hawk (1968)** - Professional skateboarder and entrepreneur.

ü **Emilio Estevez (1962)** - Actor known for his roles in "The Breakfast Club" and "The Mighty Ducks" series.

ü **Rami Malek (1981)** - Actor known for his role in TV series "Mr. Robot" and as Freddie Mercury in "Bohemian Rhapsody."

ü **Katharine Hepburn (1907)** - Iconic actress known for her strong and independent characters.

May 13th

·   **Robert Pattinson (1986)** - British actor recognized for his role as Edward Cullen in the "Twilight" series.

·   **Daphne Du Maurier (1907)** - British author known for novels like "Rebecca" and "Jamaica Inn."

·   **Stevie Wonder (1950)** - Musician and singer-songwriter known for his hits like "Superstition" and "Isn't She Lovely."

· **Lena Dunham (1986)** - Actress, filmmaker, and creator of TV series "Girls."

· **Bea Arthur (1922)** - Actress recognized for her roles in TV series "Maude" and "The Golden Girls."

May 14th

o **George Lucas (1944)** - Filmmaker known for creating the "Star Wars" and "Indiana Jones" franchises.

o **Cate Blanchett (1969)** - Australian actress known for her versatile roles and Academy Award wins.

o **Mark Zuckerberg (1984)** - Co-founder and CEO of Facebook.

o **David Byrne (1952)** - Musician, songwriter, and lead singer of the band Talking Heads.

o **Sofia Coppola (1971)** - Filmmaker known for directing films like "Lost in Translation" and "Marie Antoinette."

May 15th

§ **Andy Murray (1987)** - British professional tennis player and former world No. 1.

§ **Jamie-Lynn Sigler (1981)** - Actress recognized for her role in TV series "The Sopranos."

§ **Madeleine Albright (1937)** - Former U.S. Secretary of State and diplomat.

§ **Zara Phillips (1981)** - British equestrian and member of the royal family.

§ **George Brett (1953)** - Former MLB third baseman and Hall of Famer.

May 16th

v **Megan Fox (1986)** - Actress known for her roles in "Transformers" and "Teenage Mutant Ninja Turtles."

v **Pierce Brosnan (1953)** - Irish actor recognized for his role as James Bond in several films.

v **Janet Jackson (1966)** - Singer, songwriter, and member of the Jackson family.

v **David Boreanaz (1969)** - Actor known for his roles in TV series "Buffy the Vampire Slayer" and "Bones."

v **Tori Spelling (1973)** - Actress recognized for her role in TV series "Beverly Hills, 90210."

May 17th

Ø **Bob Saget (1956)** - Actor known for his role in TV series "Full House."

Ø **Nikki Reed (1988)** - Actress known for her roles in "Twilight" series and "Thirteen."

Ø **Trent Reznor (1965)** - Musician, singer-songwriter, and founder of Nine Inch Nails.

Ø **Tony Parker (1982)** - Former NBA player and four-time NBA champion.

Ø **Enya (1961)** - Irish singer, songwriter, and composer known for her ethereal music.

May 18th

ü **Tina Fey (1970)** - Comedian, actress, and creator of TV series "30 Rock."

ü **George Strait (1952)** - Country music singer known as the "King of Country."

ü **Yannick Noah (1960)** - Former professional tennis player and musician.

ü **Chow Yun-fat (1955)** - Hong Kong actor known for his roles in action films.

ü **Reggie Jackson (1946)** - Former MLB outfielder and Hall of Famer.

May 19th

- **Grace Jones (1948)** - Jamaican-American singer, actress, and fashion icon.

- **Sam Smith (1992)** - British singer-songwriter known for hits like "Stay with Me."

- **Malcolm X (1925)** - Civil rights activist and prominent figure in the Nation of Islam.

- **Andre the Giant (1946)** - French professional wrestler and actor.

- **Pete Townshend (1945)** - Musician, songwriter, and guitarist for The Who.

May 20th

§ **Cher (1946)** - Iconic singer, actress, and pop culture figure.

§ **Busta Rhymes (1972)** - Rapper and actor known for his energetic style.

§ **Matt Czuchry (1977)** - Actor recognized for his roles in TV series "Gilmore Girls" and "The Good Wife."

§ **James Stewart (1908)** - Legendary actor known for his roles in classic films like "It's a Wonderful Life."

§ **Timothy Olyphant (1968)** - Actor known for his roles in TV series "Justified" and "Deadwood."

May 21st

v **Notorious B.I.G. (1972)** - Rapper and songwriter known for his influential contributions to hip-hop.

v **Mr. T (1952)** - Actor, professional wrestler, and cultural icon.

v **Fats Waller (1904)** - Jazz pianist, composer, and singer known for hits like "Ain't Misbehavin'."

v **Lisa Edelstein (1966)** - Actress recognized for her roles in TV series "House" and "The West Wing."

v **Raymond Burr (1917)** - Actor known for his roles in TV series "Perry Mason" and "Ironside."

May 22nd

Ø **Sir Arthur Conan Doyle (1859)** - British author and creator of Sherlock Holmes.

Ø **Naomi Campbell (1970)** - British supermodel and actress.

Ø **Maggie Q (1979)** - Actress known for her roles in TV series "Nikita" and "Designated Survivor."

Ø **Ginnifer Goodwin (1978)** - Actress recognized for her roles in TV series "Once Upon a Time" and "Big Love."

Ø **Laurence Olivier (1907)** - British actor and director known for his Shakespearean performances.

May 23rd

ü **Drew Carey (1958)** - Comedian, actor, and host of "The Price Is Right."

ü **Jewel (1974)** - Singer-songwriter known for her folk and pop music.

ü **John Barrowman (1967)** - Scottish-American actor recognized for his role in TV series "Doctor Who" and "Torchwood."

ü **Joan Collins (1933)** - British actress known for her role in TV series "Dynasty."

ü **Maxwell (1973)** - Musician known for his soulful R&B music.

May 24th

·   **Bob Dylan (1941)** - Legendary singer-songwriter and Nobel Prize laureate.

·   **Priscilla Presley (1945)** - Actress and former wife of Elvis Presley.

·   **Jim Broadbent (1949)** - British actor known for his roles in films like "Iris" and "Moulin Rouge!"

·   **Patti LaBelle (1944)** - Singer and actress known for her powerful vocals and hits like "Lady Marmalade."

·   **John C. Reilly (1965)** - Actor recognized for his roles in "Boogie Nights" and "Chicago."

May 25th

o **Sir Ian McKellen (1939)** - British actor known for his roles as Gandalf in "The Lord of the Rings" and Magneto in "X-Men."

o **Anne Heche (1969)** - Actress recognized for her roles in films like "Donnie Brasco" and TV series "Men in Trees."

o **Mike Myers (1963)** - Canadian comedian and actor known for "Austin Powers" and "Wayne's World" series.

o **Cillian Murphy (1976)** - Irish actor recognized for his roles in "28 Days Later" and "Peaky Blinders."

o **Lauryn Hill (1975)** - Singer, rapper, and former member of the Fugees.

May 26th

§ **Stevie Nicks (1948)** - Singer-songwriter and member of the rock band Fleetwood Mac.

§ **Helena Bonham Carter (1966)** - British actress known for her roles in films like "Sweeney Todd" and "Harry Potter" series.

§ **Lenny Kravitz (1964)** - Musician and singer known for his fusion of rock, soul, and funk.

§ **Hank Williams Jr. (1949)** - Country singer known for hits like "All My Rowdy Friends Are Coming Over Tonight."

§ **Ashley Massaro (1979)** - Former WWE wrestler and reality TV contestant.

May 27th

v **Christopher Lee (1922)** - British actor known for his roles as Dracula and Saruman in "The Lord of the Rings."

v **Paul Bettany (1971)** - British actor recognized for his roles in "A Beautiful Mind" and the Marvel Cinematic Universe.

v **Joseph Fiennes (1970)** - Actor known for his roles in "Shakespeare in Love" and TV series "The Handmaid's Tale."

v **Lisa "Left Eye" Lopes (1971)** - Rapper and member of the girl group TLC.

v **André 3000 (1975)** - Rapper, singer, and member of the hip-hop duo OutKast.

May 28th

Ø **Gladys Knight (1944)** - Singer known as the "Empress of Soul" with hits like "Midnight Train to Georgia."

Ø **Kylie Minogue (1968)** - Australian pop singer known for her music and iconic music videos.

Ø **Carey Mulligan (1985) -** British actress recognized for her roles in "An Education" and "The Great Gatsby."

Ø **Rudy Giuliani (1944)** - Former Mayor of New York City and attorney.

Ø **Cameron Boyce (1999) -** Actor known for his roles in Disney Channel series and films.

May 29th

ü **John F. Kennedy (1917)** - 35th President of the United States.

ü **Annette Bening (1958)** - Actress recognized for her roles in films like "American Beauty" and "The Kids Are All Right."

ü **LaToya Jackson (1956)** - Singer, actress, and member of the Jackson family.

ü **Melissa Etheridge (1961)** - Singer-songwriter known for her rock music and activism.

ü **Rupert Everett (1959)** - British actor recognized for his roles in "My Best Friend's Wedding" and "An Ideal Husband."

May 30th

· **Idina Menzel (1971)** - Actress and singer recognized for her roles in "Rent" and voicing Elsa in "Frozen."

· **CeeLo Green (1974)** - Singer, rapper, and music producer.

· **Wynonna Judd (1964)** - Country music singer known for her solo career and as part of The Judds.

· **Colm Meaney (1953)** - Irish actor recognized for his roles in "Star Trek: The Next Generation" and "The Commitments."

· **Remy Ma (1980)** - Rapper and member of the hip-hop group Terror Squad.

May 31st

o **Clint Eastwood (1930)** - Actor, director, and filmmaker known for classics like "Dirty Harry" and "Million Dollar Baby."

o **Colin Farrell (1976)** - Irish actor known for his roles in "In Bruges" and "Phone Booth."

o **Brooke Shields (1965)** - Actress and model recognized for her roles in "The Blue Lagoon" and TV series "Suddenly Susan."

o **Tom Berenger (1949)** - Actor known for his roles in "Platoon" and "Major League."

o **Lea Thompson (1961)** - Actress recognized for her roles in "Back to the Future" and TV series "Caroline in the City."

June Birthdays

June 1st

· **Marilyn Monroe (1926)** - Iconic actress and sex symbol known for her roles in films like "Some Like It Hot."

· **Morgan Freeman (1937)** - Academy Award-winning actor known for his roles in "The Shawshank Redemption" and "Million Dollar Baby."

· **Heidi Klum (1973)** - German supermodel and television host.

· **Ron Wood (1947)** - English musician and guitarist for The Rolling Stones.

· **Amy Schumer (1981)** - Comedian and actress known for her stand-up comedy and TV show "Inside Amy Schumer."

June 2nd

o **Justin Long (1978)** - Actor known for his roles in "Dodgeball" and "Accepted."

o **Morena Baccarin (1979)** - Brazilian-American actress recognized for her roles in TV series "Firefly" and "Homeland."

o **Wentworth Miller (1972)** - Actor known for his role in TV series "Prison Break."

o **Zachary Quinto (1977)** - Actor recognized for his roles in TV series "Heroes" and as Spock in the "Star Trek" reboot films.

o **Nikki Cox (1978)** - Actress known for her roles in TV series "Unhappily Ever After" and "Las Vegas."

June 3rd

§ **Anderson Cooper (1967)** - Journalist and television personality known for his work on CNN.

§ **Rafael Nadal (1986)** - Spanish professional tennis player and multiple Grand Slam champion.

§ **Julian Marley (1975)** - Jamaican musician and reggae artist, son of Bob Marley.

§ **Paulette Goddard (1910)** - Actress known for her roles in classic films like "Modern Times" and "The Great Dictator."

o **Suzi Quatro (1950)** - American rock singer and bassist.

June 4th

v **Bar Refaeli (1985)** - Israeli supermodel and actress.

v **Russell Brand (1975)** - Comedian, actor, and author known for his stand-up comedy and film roles.

v **Joyce Meyer (1943)** - Christian author and speaker.

v **Lukas Podolski (1985) -** German former footballer and World Cup winner.

v **Scott Wolf (1968)** - Actor recognized for his role in TV series "Party of Five."

June 5th

Ø **Mark Wahlberg (1971)** - Actor, producer, and former rapper known for his roles in "The Departed" and "Ted."

Ø **Kenny G (1956)** - American saxophonist known for his smooth jazz music.

Ø **Amanda Crew (1986)** - Canadian actress recognized for her roles in TV series "Silicon Valley" and "The Haunting in Connecticut."

Ø **Suze Orman (1951)** - Financial advisor, author, and television host.

Ø **Pancho Villa (1878)** - Mexican revolutionary general.

June 6th

ü **Paul Giamatti (1967)** - Actor known for his roles in "Sideways" and "American Splendor."

ü **Kim Hyun-joong (1986)** - South Korean singer and actor, former member of SS501.

ü **Sandra Bernhard (1955)** - Comedian, actress, and singer.

ü **Robert Englund (1947)** - Actor recognized for his role as Freddy Krueger in the "A Nightmare on Elm Street" series.

ü **Steve Vai (1960)** - Guitarist and musician known for his virtuosity and solo career.

June 7th

· **Liam Neeson (1952)** - Irish actor known for his roles in "Schindler's List" and the "Taken" series.

· **Iggy Azalea (1990)** - Australian rapper and singer known for hits like "Fancy" and "Black Widow."

· **Prince (1958)** - Iconic musician, singer, and songwriter.

· **Anna Kournikova (1981)** - Former Russian professional tennis player and model.

· **Dean Martin (1917)** - Singer, actor, and member of the Rat Pack.

June 8th

○ **Kanye West (1977)** - Musician, rapper, and fashion designer.

○ **Joan Rivers (1933)** - Comedian, actress, and television host.

○ **Julianna Margulies (1966)** - Actress recognized for her roles in TV series "ER" and "The Good Wife."

○ **Frank Lloyd Wright (1867)** - Influential American architect.

○ **Nancy Sinatra (1940)** - Singer known for her hit "These Boots Are Made for Walkin'."

June 9th

§ **Johnny Depp (1963)** - Actor known for his versatile roles in "Pirates of the Caribbean" and "Edward Scissorhands."

§ **Natalie Portman (1981)** - Academy Award-winning actress known for her roles in "Black Swan" and "Star Wars" prequels.

§ **Michael J. Fox (1961)** - Actor recognized for his roles in "Back to the Future" and TV series "Family Ties."

§ **Les Paul (1915)** - Musician, inventor, and pioneer of the solid-body electric guitar.

§ **Cole Porter (1891)** - American composer and songwriter known for his classic Broadway musicals.

June 10th

v **Kate Upton (1992)** - American model and actress known for her Sports Illustrated Swimsuit Issue covers.

v **Elizabeth Hurley (1965)** - British actress and model recognized for her roles in "Austin Powers" films.

v **Judy Garland (1922)** - Iconic actress and singer known for "The Wizard of Oz" and her musical talents.

v **Gina Gershon (1962)** - Actress known for her roles in films like "Bound" and "Showgirls."

v **Shane West (1978)** - Actor recognized for his roles in TV series "ER" and "Nikita."

June 11th

Ø **Shia LaBeouf (1986)** - Actor known for his roles in "Transformers" and "Even Stevens."

Ø **Hugh Laurie (1959)** - British actor recognized for his role in TV series "House" and comedy duo with Stephen Fry.

Ø **Joshua Jackson (1978)** - Canadian actor known for his roles in TV series "Dawson's Creek" and "Fringe."

Ø **Gene Wilder (1933)** - Actor known for his roles in classic comedies like "Willy Wonka & the Chocolate Factory."

Ø **Peter Dinklage (1969)** - Actor recognized for his role as Tyrion Lannister in TV series "Game of Thrones."

June 12th

ü **Adriana Lima (1981)** - Brazilian supermodel and Victoria's Secret Angel.

ü **Dave Franco (1985)** - Actor known for his roles in "Now You See Me" and "21 Jump Street."

ü **Anne Frank (1929)** - Jewish diarist known for "The Diary of a Young Girl" documenting her experiences during the Holocaust.

ü **DJ Qualls (1978)** - Actor recognized for his roles in films like "The New Guy" and "Road Trip."

ü **Michael Muhney (1975)** - Actor known for his role in TV series "Veronica Mars."

June 13th

· **Tim Allen (1953)** - Comedian and actor known for his role in TV series "Home Improvement" and "Toy Story" franchise.

· **Chris Evans (1981)** - Actor known for his role as Captain America in the Marvel Cinematic Universe.

· **Mary-Kate and Ashley Olsen (1986)** - Twin actresses and fashion designers known for their role in "Full House."

· **Stellan Skarsgård (1951)** - Swedish actor recognized for his roles in "Good Will Hunting" and "Pirates of the Caribbean."

· **Kat Dennings (1986)** - Actress known for her role in TV series "2 Broke Girls."

June 14th

· **Yasmine Bleeth (1968)** - Actress recognized for her role in TV series "Baywatch."

· **Steffi Graf (1969)** - Former professional tennis player and multiple Grand Slam champion.

· **Boy George (1961)** - British singer-songwriter and lead vocalist of the band Culture Club.

· **Lucy Hale (1989)** - Actress and singer known for her role in TV series "Pretty Little Liars."

· **Harriet Beecher Stowe (1811)** - Author of the anti-slavery novel "Uncle Tom's Cabin."

June 15th

o **Courteney Cox (1964)** - Actress recognized for her role as Monica Geller in TV series "Friends."

o **Neil Patrick Harris (1973)** - Actor known for his roles in TV series "How I Met Your Mother" and "Doogie Howser, M.D."

o **Helen Hunt (1963)** - Academy Award-winning actress known for her roles in "As Good as It Gets" and "Mad About You."

o **Ice Cube (1969)** - Rapper, actor, and filmmaker.

o **Leah Remini (1970)** - Actress recognized for her roles in TV series "The King of Queens" and "Scientology and the Aftermath."

June 16th

§ **Tupac Shakur (1971)** - Rapper, actor, and cultural icon.

§ **John Cho (1972)** - Actor recognized for his roles in "Harold & Kumar" films and "Star Trek" series.

§ **Eddie Cibrian (1973)** - Actor known for his roles in TV series "Sunset Beach" and "Third Watch."

§ **Joyce Meyer (1943)** - Christian author and speaker.

§ **Stan Laurel (1890)** - Comedian and actor, half of the comedy duo Laurel and Hardy.

June 17th

v **Venus Williams (1980)** - Former professional tennis player and multiple Grand Slam champion.

v **Will Forte (1970)** - Comedian and actor known for his work on "Saturday Night Live" and TV series "Last Man on Earth."

v **Greg Kinnear (1963)** - Actor recognized for his roles in films like "As Good as It Gets" and "Little Miss Sunshine."

v **Newt Gingrich (1943)** - Former Speaker of the U.S. House of Representatives.

v **Barry Manilow (1943)** - Singer-songwriter known for hits like "Mandy" and "Copacabana."

June 18th

Ø **Paul McCartney (1942)** - Musician, singer-songwriter, and member of The Beatles.

Ø **Isabella Rossellini (1952)** - Actress and model known for her roles in "Blue Velvet" and "Death Becomes Her."

Ø **Blake Shelton (1976)** - Country music singer and coach on "The Voice."

Ø **Richard Madden (1986)** - Scottish actor known for his role in TV series "Game of Thrones" and "Bodyguard."

Ø **Carol Kane (1952)** - Actress recognized for her roles in films like "Annie Hall" and TV series "Taxi."

June 19th

ü **Paula Abdul (1962)** - Singer, dancer, and choreographer known for her music and judging role on "American Idol."

ü **Phylicia Rashad (1948)** - Actress recognized for her role as Clair Huxtable on TV series "The Cosby Show."

ü **Kathleen Turner (1954)** - Actress known for her roles in films like "Romancing the Stone" and "Peggy Sue Got Married."

ü **Salman Rushdie (1947)** - British-Indian novelist known for works like "Midnight's Children."

ü **Zoe Saldana (1978)** - Actress recognized for her roles in "Avatar" and the "Guardians of the Galaxy" series.

June 20th

· **Nicole Kidman (1967)** - Academy Award-winning actress known for her roles in "Moulin Rouge!" and "Big Little Lies."

· **Lionel Richie (1949)** - Singer-songwriter known for hits like "Hello" and "All Night Long."

· **John Goodman (1952)** - Actor recognized for his roles in TV series "Roseanne" and films like "The Big Lebowski."

· **Christopher Mintz-Plasse (1989)** - Actor known for his role as McLovin in "Superbad" and "Kick-Ass."

· **Olympia Dukakis (1931)** - Academy Award-winning actress known for her role in "Moonstruck."

June 21st

o **Chris Pratt (1979)** - Actor known for his roles in TV series "Parks and Recreation" and the "Guardians of the Galaxy" series.

o **Prince William (1982)** - Duke of Cambridge and member of the British royal family.

o **Lana Del Rey (1985)** - Singer-songwriter known for her dreamy pop music.

o **Juliette Lewis (1973)** - Actress and singer recognized for her roles in "Natural Born Killers" and "Cape Fear."

o **Jussie Smollett (1982)** - Actor known for his role in TV series "Empire."

June 22nd

§ **Meryl Streep (1949)** - Academy Award-winning actress known for her versatile roles in numerous films.

§ **Cyndi Lauper (1953) -** Singer-songwriter known for hits like "Girls Just Want to Have Fun" and "Time After Time."

§ **Lindsay Wagner (1949)** - Actress recognized for her role in TV series "The Bionic Woman."

§ **Carson Daly (1973)** - Television host and radio personality.

§ **Prunella Scales (1932)** - British actress recognized for her role in TV series "Fawlty Towers."

June 23rd

v **Joss Whedon (1964)** - Filmmaker and creator of TV series "Buffy the Vampire Slayer" and director of "The Avengers."

v **Selma Blair (1972)** - Actress known for her roles in "Cruel Intentions" and "Hellboy."

v **Duffy (1984)** - Welsh singer-songwriter known for her soulful music.

v **Jason Mraz (1977)** - Singer-songwriter known for hits like "I'm Yours" and "Lucky."

v Randy Jackson (1956) - Musician, producer, and former judge on "American Idol."

June 24th

Ø **Minka Kelly (1980)** - Actress recognized for her roles in TV series "Friday Night Lights" and "Parenthood."

Ø **Mindy Kaling (1979)** - Actress, comedian, and creator of TV series "The Mindy Project."

Ø **Solange Knowles (1986)** - Singer-songwriter and actress, sister of Beyoncé.

Ø **Sherry Stringfield (1967)** - Actress known for her role in TV series "ER."

Ø **Lionel Messi (1987) -** Argentine professional footballer widely regarded as one of the greatest players of all time.

June 25th

Ø **George Michael (1963)** - British singer-songwriter known for hits like "Careless Whisper" and "Faith."

Ø **Ricky Gervais (1961)** - Comedian, actor, and creator of TV series "The Office."

Ø **Carly Simon (1945)** - Singer-songwriter known for hits like "You're So Vain" and "Nobody Does It Better."

Ø **Linda Cardellini (1975)** - Actress recognized for her roles in TV series "Freaks and Geeks" and "ER."

Ø **Karisma Kapoor (1974)** - Indian actress known for her roles in Bollywood films.

June 26th

ü **Ariana Grande (1993)** - Singer and actress known for her pop music and vocal range.

ü **Chris O'Donnell (1970)** - Actor recognized for his roles in films like "Scent of a Woman" and TV series "NCIS: Los Angeles."

ü **Derek Jeter (1974)** - Former professional baseball player and New York Yankees captain.

ü **Sean Hayes (1970)** - Actor known for his role in TV series "Will & Grace."

ü **Aubrey Plaza (1984)** - Actress recognized for her roles in TV series "Parks and Recreation" and "Legion."

June 27th

·   **Tobey Maguire (1975)** - Actor known for his role as Spider-Man in the Sam Raimi film trilogy.

·   **Khloé Kardashian (1984)** - Reality TV star and entrepreneur.

·   **J.J. Abrams (1966)** - Filmmaker known for directing "Star Trek" and "Star Wars: The Force Awakens."

·   **Vera Wang (1949)** - Fashion designer known for her bridal wear.

·   **Helen Keller (1880)** - Author, activist, and lecturer who was blind and deaf.

June 28th

o **Elon Musk (1971)** - Entrepreneur and CEO of Tesla and SpaceX.

o **John Cusack (1966)** - Actor known for his roles in "Say Anything" and "High Fidelity."

o **Kathy Bates (1948)** - Academy Award-winning actress known for her roles in "Misery" and "Titanic."

o **Mel Brooks (1926)** - Filmmaker, comedian, and creator of "The Producers" and "Young Frankenstein."

o **Gilda Radner (1946)** - Comedian and actress known for her work on "Saturday Night Live."

June 29th

§ **Nicole Scherzinger (1978)** - Singer, dancer, and member of the Pussycat Dolls.

§ **Melora Hardin (1967)** - Actress recognized for her roles in TV series "The Office" and "Transparent."

§ **Gary Busey (1944)** - Actor known for his roles in "The Buddy Holly Story" and "Lethal Weapon."

§ **Lily Rabe (1982)** - Actress recognized for her roles in TV series "American Horror Story" and stage performances.

§ **Slim Pickens (1919)** - Actor known for his roles in Western films.

June 30th

v **Mike Tyson (1966)** - Former professional boxer and heavyweight champion.

v **Michael Phelps (1985)** - American swimmer and most decorated Olympian of all time.

v **Lizzy Caplan (1982)** - Actress recognized for her roles in TV series "Masters of Sex" and films like "Mean Girls."

v **Lena Horne (1917)** - Singer, actress, and civil rights activist.

v **Vincent D'Onofrio (1959)** - Actor known for his roles in "Full Metal Jacket" and TV series "Law & Order: Criminal Intent."

July Birthdays

July 1st

· **Liv Tyler (1977)** - Actress known for her roles in "Armageddon" and "The Lord of the Rings" trilogy.

· **Princess Diana (1961)** - Former wife of Prince Charles and mother of Prince William and Prince Harry.

· **Dan Aykroyd (1952)** - Actor, comedian, and member of the original cast of "Saturday Night Live."

· **Pamela Anderson (1967)** - Actress and model known for her role in TV series "Baywatch."

· **Missy Elliott (1971)** - Rapper, singer, and producer known for her innovative music.

July 2nd

○ **Margot Robbie (1990)** - Australian actress known for her roles in "The Wolf of Wall Street" and "Suicide Squad."

○ **Lindsay Lohan (1986)** - Actress and singer recognized for her roles in "Mean Girls" and "Freaky Friday."

○ **Ashley Tisdale (1985)** - Actress and singer known for her role in Disney's "High School Musical."

○ **Larry David (1947)** - Comedian, actor, and creator of TV series "Seinfeld" and "Curb Your Enthusiasm."

○ **Hermann Hesse (1877)** - German-Swiss author known for works like "Siddhartha" and "Steppenwolf."

July 3rd

§ **Tom Cruise (1962)** - Academy Award-nominated actor known for his roles in "Top Gun" and the "Mission: Impossible" series.

§ **Olivia Munn (1980)** - Actress recognized for her roles in TV series "The Newsroom" and "X-Men: Apocalypse."

§ **Julian Assange (1971)** - Australian journalist and founder of WikiLeaks.

§ **Montel Williams (1956)** - Television personality and former host of "The Montel Williams Show."

§ **Franz Kafka (1883)** - Czech writer known for his influential works of fiction.

July 4th

v **Malia Obama (1998)** - Daughter of Barack and Michelle Obama.

v **Calvin Coolidge (1872)** - 30th President of the United States.

v **Gina Lollobrigida (1927)** - Italian actress known for her roles in films like "Beat the Devil."

v **Abigail Van Buren (1918)** - Advice columnist also known as "Dear Abby."

v **Gloria Stuart (1910)** - Actress known for her role as the older Rose in "Titanic."

July 5th

Ø **Edie Falco (1963)** - Actress known for her roles in TV series "The Sopranos" and "Nurse Jackie."

Ø **Eva Green (1980)** - French actress known for her roles in "Casino Royale" and "Penny Dreadful."

Ø **Huey Lewis (1950)** - Musician and frontman of Huey Lewis and the News.

Ø **Ryan Hansen (1981)** - Actor recognized for his roles in TV series "Veronica Mars" and "Party Down."

Ø **P.T. Barnum (1810)** - Showman and circus founder known for the Barnum & Bailey Circus.

July 6th

ü **Sylvester Stallone (1946)** - Actor, writer, and director known for his roles in "Rocky" and "Rambo" series.

ü **Kevin Hart (1979)** - Comedian and actor recognized for his stand-up comedy and film roles.

ü **Geoffrey Rush (1951)** - Australian actor known for his roles in "Shine" and "Pirates of the Caribbean."

ü **Tia Mowry (1978)** - Actress recognized for her role in TV series "Sister, Sister."

ü **Janet Leigh (1927)** - Actress known for her iconic role in Alfred Hitchcock's "Psycho."

July 7th

- **Ringo Starr (1940)** - Musician and drummer for The Beatles.

- **Jim Gaffigan (1966)** - Comedian known for his stand-up comedy and observational humor.

- **Shelley Duvall (1949)** - Actress known for her roles in films like "The Shining" and "Popeye."

- **Bill Campbell (1959)** - Actor recognized for his roles in "The Rocketeer" and TV series "Once and Again."

· **Michelle Kwan (1980)** - Former figure skater and Olympic medalist.

July 8th

§ **Sophia Bush (1982)** - Actress recognized for her role in TV series "One Tree Hill" and "Chicago P.D."

§ **Beck (1970)** - Musician known for his eclectic style and hits like "Loser" and "Where It's At."

§ **Kevin Bacon (1958)** - Actor known for his roles in "Footloose" and "Apollo 13."

§ **Anjelica Huston (1951)** - Academy Award-winning actress known for her roles in "The Royal Tenenbaums" and "Prizzi's Honor."

§ **Toby Keith (1961)** - Country singer-songwriter known for hits like "Should've Been a Cowboy."

July 9th

v **Tom Hanks (1956)** - Academy Award-winning actor known for his roles in "Forrest Gump" and "Cast Away."

v **Courtney Love (1964)** - Singer-songwriter and actress, frontwoman of the band Hole.

v **Jack White (1975)** - Musician known for his roles in The White Stripes and The Raconteurs.

v **Fred Savage (1976)** - Actor known for his role in TV series "The Wonder Years."

v **Kelly McGillis (1957)** - Actress recognized for her roles in "Top Gun" and "Witness."

July 10th

Ø **Sofia Vergara (1972)** - Colombian-American actress and model known for her role in TV series "Modern Family."

Ø **Nikola Tesla (1856)** - Inventor and electrical engineer known for his contributions to modern alternating current (AC) systems.

Ø **Chiwetel Ejiofor (1977)** - Actor recognized for his roles in films like "12 Years a Slave" and "Doctor Strange."

Ø **Jessica Simpson (1980)** - Singer, actress, and fashion designer.

Ø **Neil Tennant (1954)** - Musician and singer, member of the electronic pop duo Pet Shop Boys.

July 11th

ü **Alessia Cara (1996)** - Canadian singer-songwriter known for her hit songs like "Here" and "Scars to Your Beautiful."

ü **Richie Sambora (1959)** - Musician and guitarist for the rock band Bon Jovi.

ü **Serinda Swan (1984)** - Actress recognized for her roles in TV series "Breakout Kings" and "Inhumans."

ü **Lisa Rinna (1963)** - Actress and television personality.

ü **Lil' Kim (1974)** - Rapper and singer known for her contributions to hip-hop.

July 12th

· **Malala Yousafzai (1997)** - Pakistani activist and Nobel laureate for her advocacy of education for girls.

· **Topher Grace (1978)** - Actor recognized for his role in TV series "That '70s Show" and film roles.

· **Bill Cosby (1937)** - Comedian, actor, and television producer.

· **Cheryl Ladd (1951)** - Actress recognized for her role in TV series "Charlie's Angels."

· **Michelle Rodriguez (1978)** - Actress known for her roles in "Fast & Furious" franchise and "Avatar."

July 13th

o **Harrison Ford (1942)** - Actor known for his roles in "Star Wars" and "Indiana Jones" franchises.

o **Colton Haynes (1988)** - Actor known for his roles in TV series "Teen Wolf" and "Arrow."

o **Ken Jeong (1969)** - Comedian, actor, and physician known for his roles in "The Hangover" films and "Community."

o **Cameron Crowe (1957)** - Filmmaker and director known for films like "Almost Famous" and "Jerry Maguire."

o **Patrick Stewart (1940)** - British actor recognized for his roles in "Star Trek: The Next Generation" and "X-Men" films.

July 14th

§ **Jane Lynch (1960)** - Actress known for her role in TV series "Glee" and "The Marvelous Mrs. Maisel."

§ **Phoebe Waller-Bridge (1985)** - British actress, writer, and creator of TV series "Fleabag."

§ **Ingmar Bergman (1918)** - Swedish filmmaker known for his influential films like "The Seventh Seal" and "Persona."

§ **Conor McGregor (1988)** - Irish mixed martial artist and former UFC champion.

§ **Jackie Earle Haley (1961)** - Actor known for his roles in "Watchmen" and "Little Children."

July 15th

v **Forest Whitaker (1961)** - Academy Award-winning actor known for his roles in "The Last King of Scotland" and "The Butler."

v **Diane Kruger (1976)** - German actress recognized for her roles in "Inglourious Basterds" and "Troy."

v **Brigitte Nielsen (1963)** - Danish actress and model known for her roles in "Red Sonja" and "Rocky IV."

v **Lana Parrilla (1977)** - Actress recognized for her role in TV series "Once Upon a Time."

v **Rembrandt (1606)** - Dutch painter and etcher, one of the greatest artists in history.

July 16th

Ø **Will Ferrell (1967)** - Comedian and actor known for his roles in "Anchorman" and "Talladega Nights."

Ø **Corey Feldman (1971)** - Actor known for his roles in "The Goonies" and "Stand by Me."

Ø **Rosa Salazar (1985)** - Actress recognized for her roles in "Alita: Battle Angel" and "Maze Runner."

Ø **Stewart Copeland (1952)** - Musician and drummer for the rock band The Police.

Ø **Orville Redenbacher (1907)** - American businessman and popcorn entrepreneur.

July 17th

ü **Donald Sutherland (1935)** - Canadian actor known for his roles in "MAS*H" and "The Hunger Games."

ü **Angela Merkel (1954)** - German politician and Chancellor of Germany.

ü **David Hasselhoff (1952)** - Actor recognized for his roles in TV series "Knight Rider" and "Baywatch."

ü **Luke Bryan (1976)** - Country singer-songwriter known for hits like "Country Girl (Shake It for Me)."

ü **Billie Lourd (1992)** - Actress recognized for her roles in "Star Wars" sequel trilogy and TV series "Scream Queens."

July 18th

· **Vin Diesel (1967)** - Actor known for his roles in "Fast & Furious" franchise and "xXx."

· **Kristen Bell (1980) -** Actress recognized for her roles in TV series "Veronica Mars" and "Frozen."

· **Priyanka Chopra (1982)** - Indian actress and former Miss World.

· **Nelson Mandela (1918) -** Former President of South Africa and anti-apartheid revolutionary.

· **John Glenn (1921)** - American astronaut and the first American to orbit the Earth.

July 19th

o **Benedict Cumberbatch (1976)** - British actor known for his roles in TV series "Sherlock" and "Doctor Strange."

o **Brian May (1947)** - Musician and guitarist for the rock band Queen.

o **Rosalind Franklin (1920)** - British chemist and co-discoverer of the structure of DNA.

o **Anthony Edwards (1962)** - Actor recognized for his role in TV series "ER."

o **Vikram Seth (1952) -** Indian author known for his novel "A Suitable Boy."

July 20th

§ **Sandra Oh (1971)** - Canadian actress recognized for her roles in TV series "Grey's Anatomy" and "Killing Eve."

§ **Carlos Santana (1947)** - Musician and guitarist known for his fusion of rock and Latin American music.

§ **Julianne Hough (1988) -** Dancer, actress, and former judge on "Dancing with the Stars."

§ **Gisele Bündchen (1980)** - Brazilian supermodel and philanthropist.

§ **Natalie Wood (1938)** - Actress known for her roles in films like "Rebel Without a Cause" and "West Side Story."

July 21st

v **Robin Williams (1951)** - Academy Award-winning actor known for his roles in "Good Will Hunting" and "Dead Poets Society."

v **Josh Hartnett (1978)** - Actor recognized for his roles in films like "Pearl Harbor" and "Black Hawk Down."

v **Juno Temple (1989) -** British actress known for her roles in "Atonement" and "The Dark Knight Rises."

v **Jon Lovitz (1957**) - Comedian and actor known for his work on "Saturday Night Live" and film roles.

v **Ernest Hemingway (1899)** - American novelist and Nobel Prize winner known for works like "The Old Man and the Sea."

July 22nd

Ø **Selena Gomez (1992)** - Singer, actress, and former Disney star.

Ø **Danny Glover (1946)** - Actor known for his roles in the "Lethal Weapon" series and "The Color Purple."

Ø **Willem Dafoe (1955)** - Academy Award-nominated actor known for his roles in "Platoon" and "Spider-Man."

Ø **David Spade (1964) -** Comedian and actor recognized for his roles in "Saturday Night Live" and "Tommy Boy."

Ø **Alexander Calder (1898)** - American sculptor and inventor of the mobile.

July 23rd

ü **Daniel Radcliffe (1989)** - British actor known for his role as Harry Potter in the film series.

ü **Paul Wesley (1982)** - Actor recognized for his role in TV series "The Vampire Diaries."

ü **Woody Harrelson (1961)** - Actor known for his roles in "Cheers," "The Hunger Games," and "True Detective."

ü **Philip Seymour Hoffman (1967)** - Academy Award-winning actor known for his roles in "Capote" and "The Master."

ü **Monica Lewinsky (1973)** - Former White House intern known for her involvement in the Clinton-Lewinsky scandal.

July 24th

·   **Jennifer Lopez (1969)** - Singer, actress, and dancer known for her music and film roles.

·   **Anna Paquin (1982)** - Actress recognized for her roles in films like "The Piano" and TV series "True Blood."

·   **Amelia Earhart (1897)** - Aviation pioneer and the first woman to fly solo across the Atlantic Ocean.

·   **Rose Byrne (1979)** - Australian actress known for her roles in "Bridesmaids" and "Damages."

·   **Zelda Fitzgerald (1900)** - American novelist and wife of F. Scott Fitzgerald.

July 25th

o **Matt LeBlanc (1967)** - Actor recognized for his role as Joey Tribbiani in TV series "Friends" and "Joey."

o **Rosalind Russell (1907)** - Actress known for her roles in films like "His Girl Friday" and "Auntie Mame."

o **Estelle Getty (1923)** - Actress recognized for her role as Sophia Petrillo on TV series "The Golden Girls."

o **Wendy Raquel Robinson (1967)** - Actress recognized for her role in TV series "The Game" and "The Steve Harvey Show."

o **Nate Thurmond (1941)** - Hall of Fame basketball player known for his time with the Golden State Warriors.

July 26th

§ **Sandra Bullock (1964)** - Academy Award-winning actress known for her roles in "The Blind Side" and "Speed."

§ **Kate Beckinsale (1973)** - British actress recognized for her roles in "Underworld" franchise and "Pearl Harbor."

§ **Mick Jagger (1943)** - Musician and lead vocalist of The Rolling Stones.

§ **Helen Mirren (1945)** - Academy Award-winning actress known for her versatile roles in film and television.

§ **Dorothy Hamill (1956)** - Former figure skater and Olympic gold medalist.

July 27th

v **Maya Rudolph (1972)** - Actress and comedian known for her work on "Saturday Night Live" and film roles.

v **Jonathan Rhys Meyers (1977)** - Actor recognized for his roles in TV series "The Tudors" and "Match Point."

v **Taylor Schilling (1984)** - Actress known for her role in TV series "Orange Is the New Black."

v **Julian McMahon (1968)** - Actor known for his roles in TV series "Charmed" and "Nip/Tuck."

v **Peggy Fleming (1948)** - Former figure skater and Olympic gold medalist.

July 28th

Ø **Lori Loughlin (1964)** - Actress recognized for her roles in TV series "Full House" and "When Calls the Heart."

Ø **Soulja Boy (1990)** - Rapper and record producer known for his hit single "Crank That (Soulja Boy)."

Ø **Jacqueline Kennedy Onassis (1929)** - Former First Lady of the United States and fashion icon.

Ø **Jonny Gomes (1980)** - Former Major League Baseball outfielder.

Ø **Elizabeth Berkley (1972)** - Actress recognized for her role in film "Showgirls" and TV series "Saved by the Bell."

July 29th

ü **Wil Wheaton (1972)** - Actor recognized for his roles in "Stand by Me" and "Star Trek: The Next Generation."

ü **Allison Mack (1982)** - Actress known for her role in TV series "Smallville."

ü **Dak Prescott (1993)** - Professional football quarterback for the Dallas Cowboys.

ü **Martina McBride (1966)** - Country singer-songwriter known for hits like "Independence Day."

ü **Clara Bow (1905)** - Silent film actress known as the "It Girl."

July 30th

- **Arnold Schwarzenegger (1947)** - Actor, politician, and former Governor of California.

- **Laurence Fishburne (1961)** - Actor known for his roles in "The Matrix" trilogy and "Boyz n the Hood."

- **Lisa Kudrow (1963)** - Actress recognized for her role as Phoebe Buffay on TV series "Friends."

- **Emily Brontë (1818)** - English novelist and author of the literary classic "Wuthering Heights."

- Christopher Nolan (1970) - Filmmaker known for directing "Inception," "The Dark Knight" trilogy, and more.

July 31st

o **J.K. Rowling (1965)** - British author known for the "Harry Potter" book series.

o **Wesley Snipes (1962)** - Actor recognized for his roles in "Blade" films and "White Men Can't Jump."

o **B.J. Novak (1979)** - Actor, comedian, and writer known for his work on "The Office."

o **Dean Cain (1966)** - Actor recognized for his role as Superman in TV series "Lois & Clark: The New Adventures of Superman."

o **Sherry Lansing (1944)** - Former CEO of Paramount Pictures and film producer.

August Birthdays

August 1st

·   **Jason Momoa (1979) -** Actor known for his roles in "Game of Thrones" and as Aquaman in the DC Extended Universe.

·   **Coolio (1963)** - Rapper known for hits like "Gangsta's Paradise."

·   **Sam Mendes (1965)** - Director known for films like "American Beauty" and "Skyfall."

·   **Dom DeLuise (1933)** - Comedian and actor recognized for his roles in Mel Brooks films.

·   **Yves Saint Laurent (1936)** - French fashion designer and founder of the luxury brand YSL.

August 2nd

o **Peter O'Toole (1932) -** Irish actor known for his role in "Lawrence of Arabia."

o **Mary-Louise Parker (1964)** - Actress recognized for her roles in TV series "Weeds" and "Angels in America."

o **Edward Furlong (1977)** - Actor known for his role in "Terminator 2: Judgment Day."

o **James Baldwin (1924)** - American novelist, playwright, and social critic.

o **Victoria Jackson (1959)** - Comedian and actress known for her work on "Saturday Night Live."

August 3rd

§ **Tom Brady (1977) -** American football quarterback widely considered one of the greatest in NFL history.

§ **Evangeline Lilly (1979)** - Actress known for her role as Kate Austen on TV series "Lost."

§ **Martin Sheen (1940)** - Actor known for his roles in "Apocalypse Now" and TV series "The West Wing."

§ **Martha Stewart (1941)** - Media personality, businesswoman, and former fashion model.

§ **Tony Bennett (1926)** - Legendary singer known for his classic hits.

August 4th

v **Barack Obama (1961)** - 44th President of the United States.

v **Meghan Markle (1981)** - American actress and Duchess of Sussex.

v **Billy Bob Thornton (1955)** - Actor known for his roles in "Sling Blade" and "Fargo."

v **Louis Armstrong (1901)** - Jazz trumpet player and singer.

v **Dylan Sprouse (1992)** - Actor known for his roles in "The Suite Life of Zack & Cody."

August 5th

Ø **Neil Armstrong (1930)** - American astronaut and the first person to walk on the Moon.

Ø **Maureen McCormick (1956)** - Actress recognized for her role as Marcia Brady on TV series "The Brady Bunch."

Ø **Jesse Williams (1981)** - Actor recognized for his role in TV series "Grey's Anatomy."

Ø **Loni Anderson (1945)** - Actress known for her role in TV series "WKRP in Cincinnati."

Ø **Olivia Holt (1997)** - Actress and singer known for her roles in Disney Channel shows.

August 6th

ü **M. Night Shyamalan (1970)** - Filmmaker known for directing "The Sixth Sense" and "Split."

ü **Vera Farmiga (1973)** - Actress recognized for her roles in "Up in the Air" and "The Conjuring" series.

ü **Geri Halliwell (1972)** - British singer and member of the Spice Girls.

ü **David Robinson (1965)** - Former professional basketball player, part of the "Twin Towers" with the Spurs.

ü **Lucille Ball (1911)** - Actress and comedian known for her iconic role in "I Love Lucy."

August 7th

· **Charlize Theron (1975)** - Academy Award-winning actress known for her roles in "Monster" and "Mad Max: Fury Road."

· **David Duchovny (1960)** - Actor recognized for his role in TV series "The X-Files" and "Californication."

· **Wayne Knight (1955)** - Actor known for his role as Newman on TV series "Seinfeld."

· **Carl Orff (1895) -** German composer known for his work "Carmina Burana."

· **Mata Hari (1876)** - Dutch exotic dancer and alleged spy during World War I.

August 8th

o **Dustin Hoffman (1937)** - Academy Award-winning actor known for his roles in "Rain Man" and "The Graduate."

o **Meagan Good (1981) -** Actress recognized for her roles in "Think Like a Man" and "Eve's Bayou."

o **Shawn Mendes (1998)** - Canadian singer-songwriter and pop sensation.

o **J.C. Chasez (1976)** - Singer, songwriter, and member of the boy band *NSYNC.

o **Roger Federer (1981) -** Swiss professional tennis player widely regarded as one of the greatest in history.

August 9th

§ **Whitney Houston (1963)** - Grammy Award-winning singer known for hits like "I Will Always Love You."

§ **Anna Kendrick (1985)** - Actress and singer recognized for her roles in "Pitch Perfect" and "Up in the Air."

§ **Gillian Anderson (1968)** - Actress known for her role as Dana Scully on TV series "The X-Files."

§ **Eric Bana (1968)** - Australian actor known for roles in "Hulk" and "Munich."

§ **Melanie Griffith (1957)** - Actress recognized for her roles in "Working Girl" and "Something Wild."

August 10th

v **Antonio Banderas (1960)** - Spanish actor known for his roles in "Desperado" and "The Mask of Zorro."

v **Kylie Jenner (1997)** - Reality TV star and businesswoman.

v **Rosanna Arquette (1959)** - Actress known for her roles in "Pulp Fiction" and "The Big Blue."

v **Justin Theroux (1971)** - Actor recognized for his roles in TV series "The Leftovers" and films like "The Girl on the Train."

v **Herbert Hoover (**1874) - 31st President of the United States.

August 11th

Ø **Chris Hemsworth (1983)** - Australian actor known for his role as Thor in the Marvel Cinematic Universe.

Ø **Viola Davis (1965)** - Academy Award-winning actress known for her roles in "Fences" and "The Help."

Ø **Hulk Hogan (1953)** - Former professional wrestler and cultural icon.

Ø **Chris Messina (1974) -** Actor recognized for his roles in TV series "The Mindy Project" and films like "Argo."

Ø **Steve Wozniak (1950)** - Co-founder of Apple Inc.

August 12th

ü **Casey Affleck (1975)** - Academy Award-winning actor known for his roles in "Manchester by the Sea" and "Gone Baby Gone."

ü **Cara Delevingne (1992)** - British model and actress recognized for her roles in "Suicide Squad" and "Paper Towns."

ü **Rebecca Gayheart (1971)** - Actress known for her roles in "Urban Legend" and TV series "Dead Like Me."

ü **Mark Knopfler (1949)** - Musician and co-founder of the rock band Dire Straits.

ü **George Hamilton (1939)** - Actor known for his roles in films like "Love at First Bite."

August 13th

·   **Alfred Hitchcock (1899)** - British film director known for iconic thrillers like "Psycho" and "Vertigo."

· **DeMarcus Cousins (1990)** - Professional basketball player known for his time in the NBA.

· **Sebastian Stan (1982)** - Actor recognized for his role as Bucky Barnes/Winter Soldier in the Marvel Cinematic Universe.

· **Danny Bonaduce (1959)** - Actor and radio host known for his role in TV series "The Partridge Family."

· **Annie Oakley (1860)** - American sharpshooter and exhibition shooter.

August 14th

o **Halle Berry (1966)** - Academy Award-winning actress known for her roles in "Monster's Ball" and the "X-Men" series.

o **Mila Kunis (1983)** - Actress recognized for her roles in TV series "That '70s Show" and films like "Black Swan."

o **Steve Martin (1945)** - Comedian, actor, and musician known for his comedy albums and films.

o **Magic Johnson (1959)** - Former professional basketball player and NBA legend.

o **David Crosby (1941)** - Musician and founding member of Crosby, Stills & Nash.

August 15th

§ **Jennifer Lawrence (1990)** - Academy Award-winning actress known for her roles in "The Hunger Games" and "Silver Linings Playbook."

§ **Ben Affleck (1972)** - Academy Award-winning actor known for his roles in "Argo" and "Batman v Superman."

§ **Joe Jonas (1989)** - Musician and member of the Jonas Brothers.

§ **Debra Messing (1968)** - Actress recognized for her role in TV series "Will & Grace."

§ **Napoleon Bonaparte (1769)** - Military leader and Emperor of the French.

August 16th

v **Madonna (1958)** - Iconic pop singer known for hits like "Like a Virgin" and "Material Girl."

v **Steve Carell (1962)** - Actor and comedian recognized for his role in TV series "The Office" and films like "The 40-Year-Old Virgin."

v **James Cameron (1954)** - Filmmaker known for directing "Titanic" and "Avatar."

v **Angela Bassett (1958)** - Academy Award-nominated actress known for her roles in "What's Love Got to Do with It" and "Black Panther."

v **Tim Farriss (1957)** - Musician and guitarist for the rock band INXS.

August 17th

Ø **Robert De Niro (1943)** - Academy Award-winning actor known for his roles in "Taxi Driver" and "Goodfellas."

Ø **Taika Waititi (1975)** - New Zealand filmmaker known for directing "Jojo Rabbit" and "Thor: Ragnarok."

Ø **Sean Penn (1960)** - Academy Award-winning actor known for his roles in "Mystic River" and "Milk."

Ø **Belinda Carlisle (1958)** - Singer and lead vocalist of The Go-Go's.

Ø **Donnie Wahlberg (1969)** - Actor and member of the boy band New Kids on the Block.

August 18th

ü **Robert Redford (1936)** - Academy Award-winning actor known for his roles in "Butch Cassidy and the Sundance Kid" and "The Sting."

ü **Edward Norton (1969)** - Academy Award-nominated actor known for his roles in "Fight Club" and "American History X."

ü **Christian Slater (1969)** - Actor recognized for his roles in "Heathers" and "Mr. Robot."

ü **Malcolm-Jamal Warner (1970)** - Actor recognized for his role in TV series "The Cosby Show."

ü **Andy Samberg (1978)** - Comedian, actor, and member of the comedy group The Lonely Island.

August 19th

· **John Stamos (1963)** - Actor recognized for his role as Uncle Jesse on TV series "Full House."

· **Matthew Perry (1969)** - Actor known for his role as Chandler Bing on TV series "Friends."

· **Bill Clinton (1946)** - 42nd President of the United States.

· **Kyra Sedgwick (1965)** - Actress recognized for her role in TV series "The Closer."

· **Coco Chanel (1883)** - French fashion designer and founder of the Chanel brand.

August 20th

o **Demi Lovato (1992)** - Singer and actress known for hits like "Sorry Not Sorry" and her role in "Camp Rock."

o **Amy Adams (1974)** - Academy Award-nominated actress known for her roles in "Arrival" and "American Hustle."

o **Andrew Garfield (1983)** - Actor recognized for his roles in "The Social Network" and "The Amazing Spider-Man."

o **Misha Collins (1974)** - Actor recognized for his role in TV series "Supernatural."

o **Isaac Hayes (1942)** - Musician known for his hit song "Theme from Shaft."

August 21st

§ **Usain Bolt (1986)** - Jamaican sprinter and multiple Olympic gold medalist.

§ **Hayden Panettiere (1989)** - Actress recognized for her role in TV series "Heroes."

§ **Kenny Rogers (1938)** - Country music legend known for hits like "The Gambler" and "Islands in the Stream."

§ **Carrie-Anne Moss (1967)** - Actress recognized for her role as Trinity in "The Matrix" trilogy.

§ **Wilt Chamberlain (1936)** - Former professional basketball player and NBA icon.

August 22nd

v **Kristen Wiig (1973)** - Comedian and actress known for her work on "Saturday Night Live" and films like "Bridesmaids."

v **Tori Amos (1963)** - Singer-songwriter known for her piano-driven alternative rock music.

v **Cindy Williams (1947)** - Actress recognized for her role in TV series "Laverne & Shirley."

v **James Corden (1978)** - British comedian and television host of "The Late Late Show with James Corden."

v **Dorothy Parker (1893)** - American poet, writer, and critic.

August 23rd

Ø **Kobe Bryant (1978)** - Legendary professional basketball player and NBA icon.

Ø **River Phoenix (1970)** - Actor known for his roles in "Stand by Me" and "Running on Empty."

Ø **Shelley Long (1949)** - Actress recognized for her role in TV series "Cheers."

Ø **Rick Springfield (1949)** - Musician known for his hit song "Jessie's Girl."

Ø **Gene Kelly (1912)** - Actor, dancer, and director known for his roles in classic musical films.

August 24th

ü **Rupert Grint (1988)** - British actor known for his role as Ron Weasley in the "Harry Potter" film series.

ü **Chad Michael Murray (1981)** - Actor recognized for his roles in TV series "One Tree Hill" and "Gilmore Girls."

ü **Aaliyah (1979)** - Singer and actress known for her R&B hits and roles in films like "Romeo Must Die."

ü **Dave Chappelle (1973)** - Comedian known for his stand-up specials and "Chappelle's Show."

ü **Marlee Matlin (1965)** - Academy Award-winning actress who is deaf and known for her role in "Children of a Lesser God."

August 25th

· **Tim Burton (1958)** - Filmmaker known for directing "Edward Scissorhands" and "Beetlejuice."

· **Sean Connery (1930)** - Scottish actor known for his role as James Bond in the film series.

· **Claudia Schiffer (1970)** - German supermodel and actress.

· **Alexander Skarsgård (1976) -** Swedish actor recognized for his role in TV series "True Blood" and "Big Little Lies."

· **Elvis Costello (1954)** - Musician known for his work in the punk and new wave genres.

August 26th

o **Melissa McCarthy (1970)** - Actress and comedian known for her roles in "Bridesmaids" and "Spy."

o **Macaulay Culkin (1980)** - Actor recognized for his role in the "Home Alone" film series.

o **Chris Pine (1980)** - Actor known for his role as Captain Kirk in the rebooted "Star Trek" film series.

o **Mother Teresa (1910)** - Albanian-Indian Roman Catholic nun and missionary.

o **James Harden (1989)** - Professional basketball player known for his time in the NBA.

August 27th

§ **Aaron Paul (1979)** - Actor known for his role as Jesse Pinkman in TV series "Breaking Bad."

§ **Tom Ford (1961) -** Fashion designer and film director known for his work at Gucci and Yves Saint Laurent.

§ **Sarah Chalke (1976)** - Actress recognized for her roles in TV series "Scrubs" and "Roseanne."

§ **Alexa Vega (1988)** - Actress recognized for her role in the "Spy Kids" film series.

§ **Lyndon B. Johnson (1908) -** 36th President of the United States.

August 28th

v **Jack Black (1969)** - Actor and musician known for his roles in "School of Rock" and "Tenacious D."

v **Shania Twain (1965)** - Canadian country singer known for hits like "Man! I Feel Like a Woman!" and "You're Still the One."

v **LeAnn Rimes (1982)** - Country singer who gained fame as a young artist with hit songs.

v **Armie Hammer (1986)** - Actor recognized for his roles in "Call Me by Your Name" and "The Social Network."

v **Johann Wolfgang von Goethe (1749)** - German writer and philosopher.

August 29th

Ø **Michael Jackson (1958)** - Pop music icon known as the "King of Pop."

Ø **Lea Michele (1986)** - Actress recognized for her role as Rachel Berry on TV series "Glee."

Ø **Liam Payne (1993)** - Singer and member of the boy band One Direction.

Ø **Elliott Gould (1938)** - Actor known for his roles in "MAS*H" and "Ocean's Eleven" series.

Ø **Ingrid Bergman (1915)** - Swedish actress known for her roles in classic films like "Casablanca."

August 30th

ü **Cameron Diaz (1972)** - Actress known for her roles in "There's Something About Mary" and "Charlie's Angels."

ü **Warren Buffett (1930)** - Business magnate, investor, and philanthropist.

ü **Lewis Black (1948)** - Comedian known for his stand-up specials and appearances on "The Daily Show."

ü **Bebe Rexha (1989)** - Singer-songwriter known for hits like "Meant to Be" and "I'm a Mess."

ü **Mary Shelley (1797)** - English novelist and author of the Gothic novel "Frankenstein."

August 31st

· **Richard Gere (1949)** - Actor known for his roles in "Pretty Woman" and "Chicago."

· **Chris Tucker (1971)** - Comedian and actor recognized for his roles in "Rush Hour" films.

· **Debbie Gibson (1970)** - Singer-songwriter known for her pop hits in the 1980s.

· **Jeff Hardy (1977)** - Professional wrestler and multiple-time WWE champion.

· **Maria Montessori (1870)** - Italian physician and educator known for her innovative education methods.

September Birthdays

September 1st

· **Lily Tomlin (1939)** - Emmy and Tony Award-winning actress and comedian known for her versatile performances.

· **Zendaya (1996)** - Actress and singer recognized for her roles in TV series "Euphoria" and Marvel's "Spider-Man" films.

· **Gloria Estefan (1957)** - Cuban-American singer known for hits like "Conga" and "Get On Your Feet."

· **Barry Gibb (1946)** - Musician and member of the Bee Gees.

· **Dr. Phil McGraw (1950)** - Television personality and host of "Dr. Phil."

September 2nd

o **Keanu Reeves (1964)** - Actor known for his roles in "The Matrix" trilogy and "John Wick" films.

o **Salma Hayek (1966)** - Mexican-American actress recognized for her roles in "Frida" and "Desperado."

o **Mark Harmon (1951)** - Actor known for his role as Leroy Jethro Gibbs on TV series "NCIS."

o **Jimmy Connors (1952)** - Former professional tennis player and multiple Grand Slam champion.

o **Camille Grammer (1968)** - Television personality and cast member of "The Real Housewives of Beverly Hills."

September 3rd

§ **Charlie Sheen (1965)** - Actor known for his roles in "Two and a Half Men" and films like "Platoon."

§ **Kitty Carlisle (1910)** - Actress, singer, and panelist on the TV game show "To Tell the Truth."

§ **Garrett Hedlund (1984)** - Actor known for his roles in "Tron: Legacy" and "Pan."

§ **Jennie Finch (1980)** - Former professional softball player and Olympic gold medalist.

o **Alan Ladd (1913)** - Actor known for his roles in films like "Shane" and "The Glass Key."

September 4th

v **Beyoncé (1981)** - Grammy Award-winning singer and actress known for her solo career and work with Destiny's Child.

v **Damon Wayans (1960)** - Comedian, actor, and member of the Wayans family.

v **Max Greenfield (1980)** - Actor recognized for his role as Schmidt on TV series "New Girl."

v **Mitzi Gaynor (1931)** - Actress, singer, and dancer known for her performances in musical films.

v **Whitney Port (1985)** - Television personality and cast member of "The Hills" and "The City."

September 5th

Ø **Freddie Mercury (1946)** - Legendary musician and lead vocalist of the rock band Queen.

Ø **Rose McGowan (1973)** - Actress known for her roles in TV series "Charmed" and films like "Scream."

Ø **Kat Graham (1989)** - Actress and singer recognized for her role in TV series "The Vampire Diaries."

Ø **Michael Keaton (1951)** - Academy Award-nominated actor known for his roles in "Batman" and "Birdman."

Ø **Raquel Welch (1940)** - Actress recognized for her roles in "One Million Years B.C." and "Fantastic Voyage."

September 6th

ü **Idris Elba (1972)** - Actor known for his roles in TV series "Luther" and films like "Thor" and "Beasts of No Nation."

ü **Rosie Perez (1964)** - Actress and activist known for her roles in "Do the Right Thing" and "White Men Can't Jump."

ü **Jeff Foxworthy (1958)** - Comedian known for his "You Might Be a Redneck" jokes and TV show.

ü **Swoosie Kurtz (1944)** - Emmy Award-winning actress recognized for her roles in TV series and Broadway productions.

ü **Naomie Harris (1976)** - Actress recognized for her roles in the James Bond film series and "Moonlight."

September 7th

·   **Chrissy Metz (1980)** - Actress known for her role as Kate Pearson on TV series "This Is Us."

·   **Evan Rachel Wood (1987)** - Actress recognized for her roles in TV series "Westworld" and films like "Thirteen."

·   **Eazy-E (1964)** - Rapper and co-founder of the rap group N.W.A.

·   **Buddy Holly (1936)** - Pioneer of rock and roll music with hits like "Peggy Sue" and "That'll Be the Day."

·   **Shannon Elizabeth (1973)** - Actress known for her roles in "American Pie" and "Scary Movie."

September 8th

o **Pink (1979)** - Grammy Award-winning singer known for her pop and rock hits.

o **Bernie Sanders (1941)** - U.S. Senator and former Democratic presidential candidate.

o **Patsy Cline (1932)** - Country music icon known for songs like "Crazy" and "I Fall to Pieces."

o **Jonathan Taylor Thomas (1981)** - Actor recognized for his role in TV series "Home Improvement."

o **Alek Wek (1977)** - South Sudanese-British model and fashion icon.

September 9th

§ **Adam Sandler (1966)** - Comedian and actor known for his roles in "Happy Gilmore" and "Billy Madison."

§ **Hugh Grant (1960)** - British actor known for romantic comedies like "Notting Hill" and "Four Weddings and a Funeral."

§ **Michelle Williams (1980)** - Actress recognized for her roles in "Brokeback Mountain" and "Blue Valentine."

§ **Michael Bublé (1975)** - Grammy Award-winning singer known for his modern interpretations of classic songs.

§ **Otis Redding (1941)** - Soul singer known for hits like "Sittin' On The Dock of the Bay."

September 10th

v **Colin Firth (1960)** - Academy Award-winning actor known for his roles in "The King's Speech" and "Pride and Prejudice."

v **Ryan Phillippe (1974)** - Actor recognized for his roles in "Cruel Intentions" and "Crash."

v **Amy Irving (1953)** - Actress known for her roles in films like "Carrie" and "Yentl."

v **Guy Ritchie (1968)** - Filmmaker known for directing films like "Lock, Stock and Two Smoking Barrels" and "Snatch."

v **Karl Lagerfeld (1933)** - Fashion designer and creative director of Chanel.

September 11th

Ø **Taraji P. Henson (1970)** - Academy Award-nominated actress known for her roles in "Hidden Figures" and TV series "Empire."

Ø **Harry Connick Jr. (1967)** - Musician, actor, and television host.

Ø **Ludacris (1977)** - Rapper and actor known for his hits like "What's Your Fantasy" and roles in "Fast & Furious" films.

Ø **Moby (1965)** - Musician and electronic music producer.

Ø **Bashar al-Assad (1965)** - President of Syria.

September 12th

ü **Emmy Rossum (1986)** - Actress and singer recognized for her roles in TV series "Shameless" and "The Phantom of the Opera."

ü **Jennifer Hudson (1981)** - Grammy Award-winning singer and actress known for her role in "Dreamgirls."

ü **Louis C.K. (1967)** - Comedian, actor, and filmmaker.

ü **Ian Holm (1931)** - British actor known for his roles in "The Lord of the Rings" and "Alien."

ü **Maurice Chevalier (1888)** - French actor, singer, and entertainer.

September 13th

· **Fiona Apple (1977)** - Singer-songwriter known for her album "Tidal" and hit song "Criminal."

· **Niall Horan (1993)** - Singer and member of the boy band One Direction.

· **Roald Dahl (1916)** - British author known for his children's books like "Charlie and the Chocolate Factory."

· **Tyler Perry (1969)** - Filmmaker, playwright, and actor known for his "Madea" film series.

· **Clara Schumann (1819)** - German composer and pianist of the Romantic era.

September 14th

§ **Sam Neill (1947)** - New Zealand actor known for his roles in "Jurassic Park" and "The Hunt for Red October."

§ **Andrew Lincoln (1973)** - Actor recognized for his role as Rick Grimes on TV series "The Walking Dead."

§ **Nas (1973)** - Rapper known for his influential hip-hop albums.

§ **Amy Winehouse (1983)** - Grammy Award-winning singer known for her soulful voice and hits like "Rehab."

§ **Margaret Sanger (1879)** - Birth control activist and founder of Planned Parenthood.

September 15th

v **Tom Hardy (1977)** - British actor known for his roles in "Inception," "Mad Max: Fury Road," and "Venom."

v **Prince Harry (1984)** - Member of the British royal family and Duke of Sussex.

v **Tommy Lee Jones (1946)** - Academy Award-winning actor known for his roles in "The Fugitive" and "No Country for Old Men."

v **Dan Marino (1961)** - Former professional football quarterback and NFL legend.

v **Oliver Stone (1946)** - Filmmaker known for directing movies like "Platoon" and "JFK."

September 16th

Ø **Amy Poehler (1971)** - Comedian and actress known for her work on "Saturday Night Live" and TV series "Parks and Recreation."

Ø **Nick Jonas (1992)** - Singer and member of the Jonas Brothers.

Ø **Alexis Bledel (1981)** - Actress recognized for her role in TV series "Gilmore Girls."

Ø **Lauren Bacall (1924)** - Legendary actress known for her roles in classic films like "To Have and Have Not."

Ø **Marc Anthony (1968)** - Grammy Award-winning singer known for his salsa and Latin music.

September 17th

ü **Hank Williams Sr. (1923)** - Country music icon known for hits like "Hey, Good Lookin'" and "Your Cheatin' Heart."

ü **Baz Luhrmann (1962)** - Australian filmmaker known for directing films like "Moulin Rouge!" and "Romeo + Juliet."

ü **Anne Bancroft (1931)** - Academy Award-winning actress known for her roles in "The Graduate" and "The Miracle Worker."

ü **Nate Berkus (1971)** - Interior designer and television personality.

ü **Mia Talerico (2008)** - Young actress known for her role on the Disney Channel series "Good Luck Charlie."

September 18th

· **Jada Pinkett Smith (1971)** - Actress known for her roles in films like "The Matrix" trilogy and "Girls Trip."

· **Lance Armstrong (1971)** - Former professional cyclist and seven-time winner of the Tour de France.

· **James Gandolfini (1961)** - Emmy Award-winning actor known for his role as Tony Soprano on TV series "The Sopranos."

· **Xzibit (1974)** - Rapper, actor, and television host.

· **Greta Garbo (1905)** - Swedish-American actress known for her roles in classic films like "Camille."

September 19th

o **Jimmy Fallon (1974)** - Comedian, actor, and host of "The Tonight Show Starring Jimmy Fallon."

o **Trisha Yearwood (1964)** - Country music singer known for hits like "How Do I Live" and "She's in Love with the Boy."

o **Jeremy Irons (1948)** - Academy Award-winning actor known for his roles in "The Lion King" and "Reversal of Fortune."

o **Cheri Oteri (1962)** - Comedian known for her work on "Saturday Night Live."

o **Adam West (1928)** - Actor recognized for his iconic role as Batman in the 1960s TV series.

September 20th

§ **Sophia Loren (1934)** - Academy Award-winning actress known for her roles in classic films like "Two Women" and "Marriage Italian Style."

§ **Jon Bernthal (1976)** - Actor recognized for his roles in TV series "The Walking Dead" and "The Punisher."

§ **Maggie Cheung (1964)** - Hong Kong actress known for her roles in international films.

§ **Kristen Johnston (1967)** - Actress recognized for her role in TV series "3rd Rock from the Sun."

§ **Asia Argento (1975)** - Italian actress and director known for her work in horror films.

September 21st

v **Leonard Cohen (1934)** - Canadian singer-songwriter and poet known for his deep and introspective music.

v **Maggie Grace (1983)** - Actress recognized for her roles in TV series "Lost" and the "Taken" film series.

v **Christian Serratos (1990)** - Actress known for her role as Rosita Espinosa on TV series "The Walking Dead."

v **Nicole Richie (1981)** - Television personality and fashion designer.

v **Bill Murray (1950)** - Comedian and actor known for his roles in "Ghostbusters" and "Groundhog Day."

September 22nd

Ø **Tom Felton (1987)** - British actor recognized for his role as Draco Malfoy in the "Harry Potter" film series.

Ø **Tatiana Maslany (1985)** - Actress known for her lead role in TV series "Orphan Black."

Ø **Andrea Bocelli (1958)** - Italian tenor and classical crossover artist.

Ø **Bonnie Hunt (1961)** - Actress, comedian, and talk show host.

Ø **Joan Jett (1958)** - Rock singer known for hits like "I Love Rock 'n' Roll."

September 23rd

ü **Bruce Springsteen (1949)** - Rock singer-songwriter known as "The Boss."

ü **Jason Alexander (1959)** - Actor recognized for his role as George Costanza on TV series "Seinfeld."

ü **Anthony Mackie (1978)** - Actor known for his roles in Marvel Cinematic Universe films.

ü **Julio Iglesias (1943)** - Spanish singer known for his romantic ballads.

ü **Mary Kay Place (1947)** - Actress and singer recognized for her roles in TV series "Mary Hartman, Mary Hartman" and films.

September 24th

· **Jim Henson (1936)** - Puppeteer, creator of the Muppets, and filmmaker.

· **Stephanie McMahon (1976)** - Professional wrestling personality and Chief Brand Officer of WWE.

· **Nia Vardalos (1962)** - Actress and screenwriter known for her work on "My Big Fat Greek Wedding."

· **Kevin Sorbo (1958)** - Actor recognized for his role in TV series "Hercules: The Legendary Journeys."

· **Jessica Lucas (1985)** - Actress recognized for her roles in TV series "Gotham" and "Melrose Place."

September 25th

o **Will Smith (1968)** - Actor and rapper known for his roles in "Men in Black" and "The Pursuit of Happyness."

o **Catherine Zeta-Jones (1969)** - Academy Award-winning actress known for her roles in "Chicago" and "Traffic."

o **Michael Douglas (1944)** - Academy Award-winning actor known for his roles in "Wall Street" and "Fatal Attraction."

o **Mark Hamill (1951)** - Actor recognized for his iconic role as Luke Skywalker in the "Star Wars" franchise.

o **Heather Locklear (1961)** - Actress recognized for her roles in TV series "Dynasty" and "Melrose Place."

September 26th

§ **Serena Williams (1981)** - Professional tennis player and multiple-time Grand Slam champion.

§ **Olivia Newton-John (1948)** - Australian singer and actress known for her role in "Grease."

§ **Linda Hamilton (1956)** - Actress recognized for her role as Sarah Connor in the "Terminator" film series.

§ **James Caviezel (1968)** - Actor known for his role as Jesus in "The Passion of the Christ."

§ **Christina Milian (1981)** - Singer, actress, and television personality.

September 27th

v **Gwyneth Paltrow (1972)** - Academy Award-winning actress known for her roles in "Shakespeare in Love" and the Marvel Cinematic Universe.

v **Lil Wayne (1982)** - Rapper known for his successful hip-hop career.

v **Avril Lavigne (1984)** - Singer-songwriter recognized for her punk-pop music.

v **Shaun Cassidy (1958)** - Singer, actor, and television producer.

v **Meat Loaf (1947)** - Musician known for his rock and opera-influenced music.

September 28th

Ø **Hilary Duff (1987)** - Actress and singer known for her role in TV series "Lizzie McGuire" and her music career.

Ø **Naomi Watts (1968)** - Academy Award-nominated actress known for her roles in "Mulholland Drive" and "The Ring."

Ø **Mira Sorvino (1967)** - Academy Award-winning actress recognized for her role in "Mighty Aphrodite."

Ø **Skye McCole Bartusiak (1992)** - Actress known for her roles in films like "The Patriot" and "Don't Say a Word."

Ø **Confucius (551 BC)** - Chinese philosopher and educator.

September 29th

ü **Zachary Levi (1980)** - Actor known for his role in TV series "Chuck" and for playing Shazam in the DC Extended Universe.

ü **Kevin Durant (1988)** - Professional basketball player and NBA superstar.

ü **Ian McShane (1942)** - British actor recognized for his roles in TV series "Deadwood" and "American Gods."

ü **Jerry Lee Lewis (1935)** - Rock and roll pioneer known for his energetic piano performances.

ü **Chrissy Metz (1980)** - Actress known for her role as Kate Pearson on TV series "This Is Us."

September 30th

·   **Marion Cotillard (1975)** - Academy Award-winning actress known for her roles in "La Vie en Rose" and "Inception."

·   **Fran Drescher (1957)** - Actress known for her role in TV series "The Nanny."

·   **Jenna Elfman (1971)** - Actress recognized for her roles in TV series "Dharma & Greg" and "Fear the Walking Dead."

·   **Truman Capote** (1924) - Novelist and author of "In Cold Blood" and "Breakfast at Tiffany's."

·   **Martina Hingis (1980) -** Former professional tennis player and Grand Slam champion.

October Birthdays

October 1st

·   **Julie Andrews (1935)** - Academy Award-winning actress known for her roles in "Mary Poppins" and "The Sound of Music."

·   **Zach Galifianakis (1969)** - Comedian and actor known for his roles in "The Hangover" film series.

·   **Brie Larson (1989)** - Academy Award-winning actress known for her role in "Room" and as Captain Marvel in the Marvel Cinematic Universe.

·   **Jimmy Carter (1924)** - 39th President of the United States.

·   **Randy Quaid (1950)** - Actor known for his roles in "National Lampoon's Vacation" and "Independence Day."

October 2nd

o **Sting (1951)** - Musician and lead vocalist of the rock band The Police.

o **Camilla Belle (1986)** - Actress recognized for her roles in films like "When a Stranger Calls" and "10,000 BC."

o **Kelly Ripa (1970)** - Television personality and host of "Live with Kelly and Ryan."

o **Lorraine Bracco (1954)** - Actress known for her roles in "Goodfellas" and TV series "The Sopranos."

o **Avery Brooks (1948)** - Actor recognized for his role as Captain Benjamin Sisko in TV series "Star Trek: Deep Space Nine."

October 3rd

§ **Gwen Stefani (1969)** - Singer-songwriter known for her work with No Doubt and her solo career.

§ **Tommy Lee (1962)** - Musician and drummer for the rock band Mötley Crüe.

§ **Clive Owen (1964)** - Actor known for his roles in "Closer" and "Children of Men."

§ **Lena Headey (1973)** - Actress recognized for her role as Cersei Lannister in TV series "Game of Thrones."

§ **Ashlee Simpson (1984)** - Singer-songwriter and actress.

October 4th

v **Buster Keaton (1895)** - Silent film actor and comedian known for his physical comedy.

v **Susan Sarandon (1946)** - Academy Award-winning actress known for her roles in "Thelma & Louise" and "Dead Man Walking."

v **Rachael Leigh Cook (1979)** - Actress recognized for her role in "She's All That" and "Josie and the Pussycats."

v **Liev Schreiber (1967)** - Actor known for his roles in "Ray Donovan" and "X-Men Origins: Wolverine."

v **Alicia Silverstone (1976)** - Actress known for her role in "Clueless."

October 5th

Ø **Kate Winslet (1975)** - Academy Award-winning actress known for her roles in "Titanic" and "The Reader."

Ø **Neil deGrasse Tyson (1958)** - Astrophysicist, author, and science communicator.

Ø **Guy Pearce (1967)** - Actor recognized for his roles in "Memento" and "The King's Speech."

Ø **Jesse Eisenberg (1983)** - Actor known for his roles in "The Social Network" and "Zombieland."

Ø **Bernie Mac (1957)** - Comedian and actor known for "The Bernie Mac Show" and "Ocean's Eleven."

October 6th

ü **Ioan Gruffudd (1973)** - Welsh actor recognized for his roles in "Fantastic Four" and "Horatio Hornblower" TV series.

ü **Jeremy Sisto (1974)** - Actor known for his roles in TV series "Six Feet Under" and "Suburgatory."

ü **Olivia Thirlby (1986)** - Actress recognized for her roles in "Juno" and "The Secret."

ü **Elisabeth Shue (1963)** - Actress known for her roles in "Back to the Future Part II" and "Leaving Las Vegas."

ü **Ioan Gruffudd (1973)** - Welsh actor known for his roles in "Fantastic Four" and "Horatio Hornblower."

October 7th

·   **John Mellencamp (1951)** - Musician known for hits like "Pink Houses" and "Jack and Diane."

·   **Thom Yorke (1968)** - Musician and lead vocalist of the band Radiohead.

·   **Dylan Baker (1959)** - Actor recognized for his roles in films like "Happiness" and "Spider-Man 2."

·   **Toni Braxton (1967)** - Grammy Award-winning singer known for her R&B hits.

·   **Yo-Yo Ma (1955)** - World-renowned cellist and classical musician.

October 8th

o **Matt Damon (1970)** - Academy Award-winning actor known for his roles in "Good Will Hunting" and the "Bourne" film series.

o **Sigourney Weaver (1949)** - Actress known for her iconic role in the "Alien" franchise.

o **Nick Cannon (1980)** - Comedian, actor, and television host.

o **Chevy Chase (1943)** - Comedian and actor known for his roles in "National Lampoon's Vacation" and "Community."

o **R.L. Stine (1943)** - Author known for his "Goosebumps" series of children's horror fiction.

October 9th

§ **John Lennon (1940) -** Musician and member of the Beatles.

§ **Guillermo del Toro (1964)** - Filmmaker known for directing "Pan's Labyrinth" and "The Shape of Water."

§ **Scotty McCreery (1993) -** Country music singer and winner of "American Idol" season 10.

§ **Bella Hadid (1996) -** Model recognized for her work with high-fashion brands.

§ **Tony Shalhoub (1953)** - Actor known for his roles in TV series "Monk" and "The Marvelous Mrs. Maisel."

October 10th

v **Mario Lopez (1973) -** Actor and television host known for his role in TV series "Saved by the Bell."

v **Dan Stevens (1982)** - British actor recognized for his roles in TV series "Downton Abbey" and "Legion."

v **Bai Ling (1966) -** Chinese-American actress known for her roles in "The Crow" and "Red Corner."

v **David Lee Roth (1954)** - Musician and lead vocalist of the rock band Van Halen.

v **Mýa (1979)** - Singer and actress known for her R&B and pop music.

October 11th

Ø **Joan Cusack (1962)** - Actress known for her roles in films like "Working Girl" and "School of Rock."

Ø **Michelle Trachtenberg (1985)** - Actress recognized for her roles in "Buffy the Vampire Slayer" and "Gossip Girl."

Ø **Luke Perry (1966)** - Actor known for his role as Dylan McKay on TV series "Beverly Hills, 90210."

Ø **Cardi B (1992)** - Rapper known for her chart-topping hits and energetic personality.

Ø **Eleanor Roosevelt (1884) -** Former First Lady of the United States and human rights activist.

October 12th

ü **Hugh Jackman (1968)** - Actor known for his role as Wolverine in the "X-Men" film series and his work on Broadway.

ü **Bode Miller (1977) -** Former World Cup alpine ski racer and Olympic gold medalist.

ü **Josh Hutcherson (1992)** - Actor known for his role as Peeta Mellark in "The Hunger Games" film series.

ü **Kirk Cameron (1970)** - Actor known for his role in TV series "Growing Pains."

ü **Luciano Pavarotti (1935)** - Operatic tenor known for his powerful voice and performances.

October 13th

·   **Sacha Baron Cohen (1971)** - Comedian and actor known for his characters Ali G and Borat.

·   **Ashanti (1980)** - Singer-songwriter known for her R&B hits.

·   **Marie Osmond (1959)** - Singer, actress, and member of the Osmonds musical group.

·   **Kelly Preston (1962)** - Actress recognized for her roles in "Jerry Maguire" and "Twins."

·   **Nancy Kerrigan (1969)** - Former figure skater and Olympic medalist.

October 14th

o **Usher (1978)** - Grammy Award-winning singer known for his R&B and pop music.

o **Mia Wasikowska (1989)** - Australian actress recognized for her roles in "Alice in Wonderland" and "Jane Eyre."

o **Stacy Keibler (1979)** - Former professional wrestler and actress.

o **Steve Coogan (1965)** - British comedian and actor known for his character Alan Partridge.

o **Ralph Lauren (1939)** - Fashion designer and founder of the Ralph Lauren Corporation.

October 15th

§ **Emeril Lagasse (1959)** - Celebrity chef and television personality.

§ **Bailee Madison (1999)** - Actress recognized for her roles in TV series "Good Witch" and "Bridge to Terabithia."

§ **Sarah Ferguson (1959)** - Duchess of York and member of the British royal family.

§ **Penny Marshall (1943)** - Actress and director known for her role in "Laverne & Shirley" and directing "Big."

§ **Mario Puzo (1920)** - Author known for his novel "The Godfather."

October 16th

v **Angela Lansbury (1925)** - Actress known for her roles in TV series "Murder, She Wrote" and "Beauty and the Beast."

v **Tim Robbins (1958)** - Actor, director, and Academy Award winner.

v **John Mayer (1977)** - Musician known for his pop and rock music.

v **Kellie Martin (1975)** - Actress recognized for her roles in TV series "Life Goes On" and "ER."

v **Caterina Scorsone (1981)** - Actress known for her role in TV series "Grey's Anatomy."

October 17th

Ø **Eminem (1972)** - Grammy Award-winning rapper known for his hit songs and albums.

Ø **Felicity Jones (1983)** - British actress recognized for her roles in "The Theory of Everything" and "Rogue One."

Ø **Wyclef Jean (1969)** - Musician known for his work with the hip-hop group The Fugees.

Ø **Norm MacDonald (1959)** - Comedian and actor known for his time on "Saturday Night Live."

Ø **Rita Hayworth (1918)** - Golden Age actress known for her roles in classic films.

October 18th

ü **Zac Efron (1987)** - **Actor** and singer recognized for his roles in the "High School Musical" franchise and other films.

ü **Jean-Claude Van Damme (1960)** - Belgian actor known for his roles in action films like "Bloodsport" and "Kickboxer."

ü **Lindsey Vonn (1984)** - Former World Cup alpine ski racer and Olympic gold medalist.

ü **Tyler Posey (1991)** - Actor recognized for his role in TV series "Teen Wolf."

ü **Freida Pinto (1984)** - Indian actress known for her role in "Slumdog Millionaire."

October 19th

· **John Lithgow (1945)** - Actor known for his roles in TV series "3rd Rock from the Sun" and films like "The World According to Garp."

· **Jon Favreau (1966)** - Filmmaker, actor, and director known for "Iron Man" and "The Jungle Book."

· **Evander Holyfield (1962)** - Former professional boxer and multiple-time heavyweight champion.

· **Trey Parker (1969)** - Co-creator of the animated TV series "South Park."

· **Joy Behar (1942) -** Television host and comedian known for her work on "The View."

October 20th

o **Snoop Dogg (1971)** - Rapper and songwriter known for his contributions to hip-hop.

o **Viggo Mortensen (1958)** - Actor known for his roles in "The Lord of the Rings" trilogy and "Green Book."

o **Tom Petty (1950)** - Musician and lead vocalist of Tom Petty and the Heartbreakers.

o **Dannii Minogue (1971)** - Australian singer, actress, and television personality.

o **Kamala Harris (1964) -** 49th Vice President of the United States.

October 21st

§ **Kim Kardashian (1980)** - Television personality, socialite, and businesswoman.

§ **Amber Rose (1983) -** Model, actress, and activist.

§ **Judge Judy Sheindlin (1942)** - Television personality and former family court judge.

§ **Ken Watanabe (1959) -** Japanese actor known for his roles in "The Last Samurai" and "Inception."

§ **Carrie Fisher (1956)** - Actress known for her iconic role as Princess Leia in the "Star Wars" franchise.

October 22nd

v **Christopher Lloyd (1938)** - Actor recognized for his role as Doc Brown in the "Back to the Future" trilogy.

v **Jeff Goldblum (1952)** - Actor known for his roles in "Jurassic Park" and "Independence Day."

v **Jesse Tyler Ferguson (1975)** - Actor recognized for his role in TV series "Modern Family."

v **Annette Funicello (1942)** - Actress and singer known for her roles in Disney films and the "Mickey Mouse Club."

v **Shaggy (1968)** - Jamaican musician known for his reggae and dancehall music.

October 23rd

Ø **Ryan Reynolds (1976)** - Actor known for his roles in "Deadpool" and "The Proposal."

Ø **Emilia Clarke (1986) -** British actress recognized for her role as Daenerys Targaryen in TV series "Game of Thrones."

Ø **Cat Deeley (1976)** - Television presenter and host of "So You Think You Can Dance."

Ø **Weird Al Yankovic (1959)** - Musician and comedian known for his humorous song parodies.

Ø **Ang Lee (1954)** - Filmmaker known for directing films like "Brokeback Mountain" and "Life of Pi."

October 24th

ü **Drake (1986) -** Grammy Award-winning rapper and musician.

ü **PewDiePie (1989)** - Swedish YouTuber known for his gaming videos.

ü **Casey Wilson (1980)** - Actress and comedian recognized for her role in TV series "Happy Endings."

ü **Kevin Kline (1947)** - Academy Award-winning actor known for his roles in "A Fish Called Wanda" and "Dave."

ü **Mallika Sherawat (1976)** - Indian actress known for her work in Bollywood films.

October 25th

· **Katy Perry (1984)** - Grammy-nominated singer known for her pop music hits.

· **Pablo Picasso (1881) -** Spanish painter and one of the most influential artists of the 20th century.

· **Craig Robinson (1971) -** Actor and comedian known for his roles in "The Office" and "Hot Tub Time Machine."

· **Adam Goldberg (1970)** - Actor recognized for his roles in "Dazed and Confused" and "Saving Private Ryan."

· **Ciara (1985)** - Singer-songwriter known for her R&B and pop music.

October 26th

o **Hillary Clinton (1947)** - Former First Lady, Secretary of State, and presidential candidate.

o **Keith Urban (1967)** - Country music singer-songwriter and Grammy Award winner.

o **Dylan McDermott (1961)** - Actor recognized for his roles in TV series "The Practice" and "American Horror Story."

o **Jon Heder (1977)** - Actor known for his role in "Napoleon Dynamite."

o **Seth MacFarlane (1973)** - Animator, comedian, and creator of "Family Guy."

October 27th

§ **Kelly Osbourne (1984)** - Television personality, singer, and fashion designer.

§ Vanessa Mae (1978) - British violinist known for her fusion of classical music with pop and electronic genres.

§ Dylan Baker (1959) - Actor recognized for his roles in "Happiness" and "Spider-Man 2."

§ John Cleese (1939) - British comedian, actor, and member of Monty Python.

§ **Marla Maples (1963)** - Actress and former wife of Donald Trump.

October 28th

v **Julia Roberts (1967)** - Academy Award-winning actress known for her roles in "Pretty Woman" and "Erin Brockovich."

v **Joaquin Phoenix (1974)** - Academy Award-winning actor known for his roles in "Joker" and "Walk the Line."

v **Bill Gates (1955)** - Co-founder of Microsoft and philanthropist.

v **Matt Smith (1982)** - British actor recognized for his role as the Eleventh Doctor in "Doctor Who."

v **Lauren Holly (1963)** - Actress known for her roles in TV series "Picket Fences" and "NCIS."

October 29th

v **Winona Ryder (1971)** - Actress known for her roles in "Beetlejuice" and "Stranger Things."

v **Gabrielle Union (1972)** - Actress recognized for her roles in "Bring It On" and "Being Mary Jane."

v **Tracee Ellis Ross (1972)** - Actress known for her role in TV series "Black-ish."

v **India.Arie (1975)** - Grammy Award-winning singer-songwriter known for her soul and R&B music.

v **Richard Dreyfuss (1947)** - Academy Award-winning actor known for his roles in "Jaws" and "Close Encounters of the Third Kind."

October 30th

Ø **Ivanka Trump (1981)** - Businesswoman, former Senior Advisor to the President, and daughter of Donald Trump.

Ø **Nia Long (1970)** - Actress known for her roles in "Boyz n the Hood" and "The Best Man."

Ø **Matthew Morrison (1978)** - Actor recognized for his role in TV series "Glee."

Ø **Henry Winkler (1945)** - Actor known for his role as Fonzie on TV series "Happy Days."

Ø **Ezra Pound (1885)** - American poet and critic.

October 31st

ü **Vanilla Ice (1967)** - Rapper and actor known for his hit song "Ice Ice Baby."

ü **Peter Jackson (1961)** - Filmmaker known for directing "The Lord of the Rings" film trilogy.

ü **Rob Schneider (1963)** - Comedian and actor recognized for his roles in "Saturday Night Live" and films like "Deuce Bigalow."

ü **Willow Smith (2000)** - Singer, actress, and daughter of actors Will Smith and Jada Pinkett Smith.

ü **Dan Rather (1931)** - Former CBS Evening News anchor and journalist.

November Birthdays

November 1st

- **Penn Badgley (1986)** - Actor recognized for his role in TV series "Gossip Girl" and "You."

- **Jenny McCarthy (1972)** - Television personality, actress, and former co-host of "The View."

- **Toni Collette (1972)** - Actress known for her roles in "The Sixth Sense" and "Little Miss Sunshine."

- **Aishwarya Rai Bachchan (1973)** - Indian actress and former Miss World.

- **Lyle Lovett (1957)** - Singer-songwriter known for his country and folk music.

November 2nd

- **David Schwimmer (1966)** - Actor known for his role as Ross Geller on TV series "Friends."

- **Shah Rukh Khan (1965)** - Indian actor and film producer, often referred to as the "King of Bollywood."

- **Nelly (1974)** - Rapper and singer known for hits like "Hot in Herre" and "Dilemma."

- **Kendall Jenner (1995)** - Model and television personality from the Kardashian-Jenner family.

- **K. D. Lang (1961)** - Canadian singer-songwriter known for her country and pop music.

November 3rd

§ **Dolph Lundgren (1957)** - Swedish actor known for his roles in action films like "Rocky IV" and "Universal Soldier."

§ **Kendall Schmidt (1990)** - Musician and actor recognized for his role in TV series "Big Time Rush."

§ **Anna Wintour (1949)** - Editor-in-chief of Vogue magazine and influential figure in the fashion industry.

§ **Roseanne Barr (1952)** - Comedian, actress, and creator of the TV series "Roseanne."

§ **Kendall Jenner (1995)** - Model and television personality from the Kardashian-Jenner family.

November 4th

v **Matthew McConaughey (1969)** - Academy Award-winning actor known for his roles in "Dallas Buyers Club" and "Interstellar."

v **Sean "Diddy" Combs (1969)** - Rapper, entrepreneur, and music producer.

v **Kathy Griffin (1960)** - Comedian, actress, and television host.

v **Ralph Macchio (1961) -** Actor recognized for his role in "The Karate Kid" film series.

v **Loretta Swit (1937)** - Actress known for her role as Major Margaret "Hot Lips" Houlihan on TV series "MAS*H."

November 5th

Ø **Kris Jenner (1955)** - Television personality and matriarch of the Kardashian-Jenner family.

Ø **Bryan Adams (1959)** - Canadian singer-songwriter known for hits like "Summer of '69" and "(Everything I Do) I Do It for You."

Ø **Tatum O'Neal (1963)** - Actress and Academy Award winner.

Ø **Famke Janssen (1964)** - Dutch actress recognized for her roles in "X-Men" and "GoldenEye."

Ø **Kevin Jonas (1987)** - Musician and member of the pop-rock band Jonas Brothers.

November 6th

ü **Emma Stone (1988)** - Academy Award-winning actress known for her roles in "La La Land" and "The Help."

ü **Ethan Hawke (1970) -** Actor, writer, and director known for his roles in films like "Training Day" and "Boyhood."

ü **Rebecca Romijn (1972)** - Actress and former model recognized for her role as Mystique in the "X-Men" film series.

ü **Sally Field (1946) -** Academy Award-winning actress known for her roles in "Norma Rae" and "Forrest Gump."

ü **Thandie Newton (1972)** - Actress known for her roles in films like "Crash" and TV series "Westworld."

November 7th

- **Adam Devine (1983)** - Actor and comedian known for his roles in "Pitch Perfect" and TV series "Workaholics."

- **Joni Mitchell (1943)** - Singer-songwriter and influential figure in folk and rock music.

- **David Guetta (1967)** - French DJ and music producer known for his electronic dance music.

- **Jason London (1972)** - Actor recognized for his roles in "Dazed and Confused" and "Out Cold."

- **Billy Graham (1918)** - American evangelist and preacher.

November 8th

o **Gordon Ramsay (1966)** - Celebrity chef, television personality, and restaurateur.

o **Tara Reid (1975)** - Actress recognized for her roles in "American Pie" and "Sharknado."

o **Parker Posey (1968)** - Actress known for her roles in independent films and "Dazed and Confused."

o **Leif Garrett (1961)** - Former teen idol and singer.

o **Alfre Woodard (1952)** - Actress known for her roles in "Cross Creek" and "12 Years a Slave."

November 9th

§ **Carl Sagan (1934)** - Astronomer, astrophysicist, and science communicator.

§ **Lou Ferrigno (1951)** - Actor and former professional bodybuilder known for his role as the Hulk in the TV series "The Incredible Hulk."

§ **French Montana (1984)** - Rapper and songwriter.

§ **Eric Dane (1972)** - Actor recognized for his roles in TV series "Grey's Anatomy" and "The Last Ship."

§ **Vanessa Minnillo (1980)** - Television personality and former Miss Teen USA.

November 10th

v **Mackenzie Foy (2000)** - Actress known for her roles in "The Twilight Saga" and "Interstellar."

v **Tracy Morgan (1968) -** Comedian and actor recognized for his role in TV series "30 Rock" and "Saturday Night Live."

v **Ellen Pompeo (1969)** - Actress known for her role as Meredith Grey in TV series "Grey's Anatomy."

v **Brittany Murphy (1977)** - Actress known for her roles in "Clueless" and "8 Mile."

v **Roy Scheider (1932) -** Actor known for his roles in "Jaws" and "All That Jazz."

November 11th

Ø **Leonardo DiCaprio (1974)** - Academy Award-winning actor known for his roles in "Titanic" and "The Revenant."

Ø **Demi Moore (1962)** - Actress recognized for her roles in "Ghost" and "A Few Good Men."

Ø **Calista Flockhart (1964)** - Actress known for her role in TV series "Ally McBeal."

Ø **Stanley Tucci (1960) -** Actor known for his roles in "The Devil Wears Prada" and "The Hunger Games."

Ø **Christa B. Allen (1991)** - Actress recognized for her role in TV series "Revenge."

November 12th

ü **Anne Hathaway (1982)** - Academy Award-winning actress known for her roles in "The Princess Diaries" and "Les Misérables."

ü **Ryan Gosling (1980)** - Actor known for his roles in "La La Land" and "The Notebook."

ü **Neil Young (1945)** - Musician and singer-songwriter known for his contributions to rock and folk music.

ü **Omarion (1984)** - R&B singer and former member of the boy band B2K.

ü **Tonya Harding (1970) -** Former figure skater and Olympic competitor.

November 13th

· **Whoopi Goldberg (1955) -** Actress, comedian, and television host known for her work on "The View."

· **Gerard Butler (1969) -** Actor recognized for his roles in "300" and "The Phantom of the Opera."

· **Jimmy Kimmel (1967) -** Comedian and television host of "Jimmy Kimmel Live!"

· **Monique Coleman (1980) -** Actress recognized for her role in "High School Musical."

· **Robert Louis Stevenson (1850) -** Scottish author known for classics like "Treasure Island" and "Strange Case of Dr Jekyll and Mr Hyde."

November 14th

o **Prince Charles (1948) -** Heir apparent to the British throne and Prince of Wales.

o **Josh Duhamel (1972) -** Actor recognized for his roles in TV series "Las Vegas" and the "Transformers" film series.

o **Yanni (1954) -** Greek composer known for his contemporary instrumental music.

o **Olga Kurylenko (1979) -** Ukrainian-French actress recognized for her role in the James Bond film "Quantum of Solace."

o **Condoleezza Rice (1954) -** Former United States Secretary of State and diplomat.

November 15th

§ **Chad Kroeger (1974) -** Musician and lead vocalist of the rock band Nickelback.

§ **Ed Asner (1929) -** Actor known for his roles in TV series "The Mary Tyler Moore Show" and "Lou Grant."

§ **Shailene Woodley (1991) -** Actress known for her roles in "The Fault in Our Stars" and "Big Little Lies."

§ **Sean Murray (1977) -** Actor recognized for his role in TV series "NCIS."

§ **Petula Clark (1932) -** British singer-songwriter known for hits like "Downtown."

November 16th

v **Maggie Gyllenhaal (1977) -** Actress known for her roles in "The Dark Knight" and "Secretary."

v **Lisa Bonet (1967) -** Actress recognized for her role as Denise Huxtable on TV series "The Cosby Show."

v **Owen Wilson (1968)** - Actor known for his roles in "Wedding Crashers" and "Zoolander."

v **Brandi Glanville (1972)** - Television personality and former cast member of "The Real Housewives of Beverly Hills."

v **Gemma Atkinson (1984)** - British actress and model known for her work on TV series "Hollyoaks."

November 17th

Ø **Rachel McAdams (1978)** - Actress known for her roles in "The Notebook" and "Mean Girls."

Ø **Danny DeVito (1944)** - Actor, comedian, and filmmaker known for his roles in "Matilda" and "It's Always Sunny in Philadelphia."

Ø **RuPaul (1960) -** Drag queen, singer, and host of "RuPaul's Drag Race."

Ø **Sophie Marceau (1966)** - French actress recognized for her roles in "Braveheart" and "The World Is Not Enough."

Ø **Lauren Hutton (1943)** - Model and actress known for her iconic gap-toothed smile.

November 18th

ü **Owen Wilson (1968)** - Actor known for his roles in "Wedding Crashers" and "Zoolander."

ü **David Ortiz (1975)** - Former professional baseball player and designated hitter.

ü **Chloe Sevigny (1974)** - Actress known for her roles in independent films like "Boys Don't Cry" and "Kids."

ü **Nas (1973)** - Rapper and songwriter known for his contributions to hip-hop.

ü **Linda Evans** (1942) - Actress recognized for her role in TV series "Dynasty."

November 19th

· **Jodie Foster (1962)** - Academy Award-winning actress known for her roles in "The Silence of the Lambs" and "Panic Room."

· **Meg Ryan (1961)** - Actress recognized for her roles in romantic comedies like "When Harry Met Sally" and "Sleepless in Seattle."

· **Larry King (1933) -** Television and radio host known for "Larry King Live."

· **Adam Driver (1983)** - Actor known for his roles in TV series "Girls" and films like "Star Wars: The Force Awakens."

· **Allison Janney (1959)** - Actress recognized for her roles in TV series "The West Wing" and "Mom."

November 20th

o **Joe Biden (1942)** - 46th President of the United States.

o **Dierks Bentley (1975)** - Country music singer-songwriter known for hits like "Drunk on a Plane" and "Somewhere on a Beach."

o **Josh Turner (1977)** - Country music singer known for his deep voice and hits like "Your Man" and "Long Black Train."

o **Bo Derek (1956)** - Actress recognized for her roles in films like "10" and "Bolero."

o **Ming-Na Wen (1963)** - Actress known for her roles in "Mulan" and TV series "Agents of S.H.I.E.L.D."

November 21st

§ **Goldie Hawn (1945)** - Academy Award-winning actress known for her roles in "Cactus Flower" and "Private Benjamin."

§ **Jena Malone (1984)** - Actress recognized for her roles in "Donnie Darko" and "The Hunger Games" film series.

§ **Nicollette Sheridan (1963)** - Actress known for her role on TV series "Desperate Housewives."

§ **Voltaire (1694)** - French writer and philosopher.

§ **Colleen Ballinger (1986)** - YouTuber and comedian known for her character "Miranda Sings."

November 22nd

v **Scarlett Johansson (1984)** - Actress known for her roles in "Lost in Translation" and the Marvel Cinematic Universe.

v **Jamie Lee Curtis (1958)** - Actress recognized for her roles in "Halloween" and "True Lies."

v **Mark Ruffalo (1967)** - Actor known for his role as Hulk in the Marvel Cinematic Universe.

v **Boris Becker (1967) -** Former professional tennis player and Wimbledon champion.

v **Mads Mikkelsen (1965)** - Danish actor recognized for his roles in "Casino Royale" and TV series "Hannibal."

November 23rd

Ø **Miley Cyrus (1992)** - Singer-songwriter and actress known for her pop and country music.

Ø **Nicole "Snooki" Polizzi (1987)** - Television personality and former cast member of "Jersey Shore."

Ø **Oded Fehr (1970)** - Actor recognized for his roles in "The Mummy" film series and TV series "Covert Affairs."

Ø **Bruce Hornsby (1954)** - Musician and singer known for his hit song "The Way It Is."

Ø **Boris Karloff (1887)** - Actor known for his role as Frankenstein's monster in the classic film.

November 24th

ü **Sarah Hyland (1990)** - Actress recognized for her role in TV series "Modern Family."

ü **Katherine Heigl (1978)** - Actress known for her roles in "Grey's Anatomy" and "Knocked Up."

ü **Colin Hanks (1977)** - Actor recognized for his roles in TV series "Fargo" and "Life in Pieces."

ü **Denise Crosby (1957)** - Actress known for her role as Tasha Yar on TV series "Star Trek: The Next Generation."

ü **Pete Best (1941)** - Former drummer of the Beatles before Ringo Starr.

November 25th

·   **Christina Applegate (1971)** - Actress recognized for her roles in TV series "Married... with Children" and "Dead to Me."

·   **Joe DiMaggio (1914)** - Former professional baseball player and New York Yankees legend.

·   **Katie Cassidy (1986)** - Actress known for her roles in TV series "Arrow" and "Supernatural."

·   **Dougray Scott (1965)** - Scottish actor recognized for his roles in films like "Mission: Impossible 2."

· **John F. Kennedy Jr. (1960)** - Lawyer, journalist, and son of President John F. Kennedy.

November 26th

o **Tina Turner (1939)** - Singer and rock icon known for hits like "Proud Mary" and "What's Love Got to Do with It."

o **DJ Khaled (1975)** - Record producer, DJ, and music executive.

o **Natasha Bedingfield (1981)** - British singer-songwriter known for hits like "Unwritten" and "Pocketful of Sunshine."

o **Rita Ora (1990)** - Singer, actress, and television personality.

o **Rich Little (1938)** - Impressionist and comedian known for his celebrity impressions.

November 27th

§ **Bruce Lee (1940)** - Martial artist, actor, and cultural icon.

§ **Jaleel White (1976)** - Actor recognized for his role as Steve Urkel on TV series "Family Matters."

§ **Robin Givens (1964)** - Actress known for her roles in TV series "Head of the Class" and "Riverdale."

§ **Michael Vartan (1968)** - Actor recognized for his role in TV series "Alias."

§ **James Avery (1945)** - Actor known for his role as Uncle Phil on TV series "The Fresh Prince of Bel-Air."

November 28th

v **Jon Stewart (1962)** - Comedian, writer, and former host of "The Daily Show."

v **Karen Gillan (1987)** - Scottish actress recognized for her role as Nebula in the Marvel Cinematic Universe.

v **Anna Nicole Smith (1967)** - Model and actress known for her Playboy appearances and reality TV show.

v **Ed Harris (1950)** - Academy Award-nominated actor known for his roles in "Apollo 13" and "The Truman Show."

v **Mary Elizabeth Winstead (1984)** - Actress recognized for her roles in "Scott Pilgrim vs. the World" and "10 Cloverfield Lane."

November 29th

Ø **Anna Faris (1976)** - Actress known for her roles in "Scary Movie" and TV series "Mom."

Ø **Don Cheadle (1964)** - Academy Award-nominated actor recognized for his roles in "Hotel Rwanda" and "Iron Man."

Ø **Lucas Black (1982) -** Actor known for his roles in films like "Sling Blade" and "The Fast and the Furious: Tokyo Drift."

Ø **Chuck Schumer (1950)** - United States Senator from New York.

Ø **Howie Mandel (1955) -** Comedian, actor, and television host known for "Deal or No Deal."

November 30th

ü **Chrissy Teigen (1985) -** Model, television personality, and cookbook author.

ü **Kaley Cuoco (1985) -** Actress recognized for her role as Penny in TV series "The Big Bang Theory."

ü **Bo Jackson (1962) -** Former professional baseball and football player, known for his athleticism.

ü **Mandy Patinkin (1952)** - Actor known for his roles in "The Princess Bride" and TV series "Homeland."

ü **Winston Churchill (1874)** - Former Prime Minister of the United Kingdom and statesman.

December Birthdays

December 1st

· **Woody Allen (1935) -** Filmmaker, actor, and comedian known for films like "Annie Hall" and "Midnight in Paris."

· **Sarah Silverman (1970) -** Comedian, actress, and writer known for her stand-up and TV series "The Sarah Silverman Program."

· **Bette Midler (1945) -** Singer, actress, and entertainer known for hits like "Wind Beneath My Wings."

· **Zoe Kravitz (1988) -** Actress and singer recognized for her roles in "Big Little Lies" and "Fantastic Beasts."

· **Richard Pryor (1940) -** Comedian and actor known for his groundbreaking stand-up comedy and films.

December 2nd

o **Britney Spears (1981) -** Pop singer known for hits like "Baby One More Time" and "Toxic."

o **Lucy Liu (1968) -** Actress known for her roles in TV series "Ally McBeal" and the "Charlie's Angels" films.

o **Nelly Furtado (1978) -** Singer-songwriter known for hits like "I'm Like a Bird" and "Promiscuous."

o **Aaron Rodgers (1983) -** Professional American football quarterback for the Green Bay Packers.

o **Charlie Puth (1991) -** Singer-songwriter known for his pop and R&B music.

December 3rd

§ **Brendan Fraser (1968) -** Actor known for his roles in "The Mummy" film series and "George of the Jungle."

§ **Julianne Moore (1960) -** Academy Award-winning actress recognized for her roles in "Still Alice" and "Boogie Nights."

§ **Amanda Seyfried (1985) -** Actress known for her roles in "Mean Girls" and "Mamma Mia!"

§ **Ozzy Osbourne (1948) -** Rock icon and lead vocalist of the band Black Sabbath.

§ **Anna Chlumsky (1980) -** Actress recognized for her role in TV series "Veep."

December 4th

v **Tyra Banks (1973)** - Model, television personality, and businesswoman.

v **Jay-Z (1969)** - Rapper, songwriter, and entrepreneur.

v **Marisa Tomei (1964)** - Academy Award-winning actress known for her roles in "My Cousin Vinny" and "The Wrestler."

v **Jeff Bridges (1949)** - Academy Award-winning actor known for his roles in "The Big Lebowski" and "Crazy Heart."

v **Orlando Brown (1987)** - Actor known for his role in TV series "That's So Raven."

December 5th

ü **Walt Disney (1901)** - Entrepreneur, animator, and co-founder of The Walt Disney Company.

ü **Frankie Muniz (1985)** - Actor known for his role in TV series "Malcolm in the Middle."

ü **Keri Hilson (1982)** - Singer-songwriter known for her R&B and pop music.

ü **Paula Patton (1975)** - Actress recognized for her roles in "Precious" and "Mission: Impossible - Ghost Protocol."

ü **Lauren London (1984)** - Actress known for her roles in "ATL" and "The Game."

December 6th

ü **Judd Apatow (1967)** - Filmmaker, comedian, and producer known for comedies like "The 40-Year-Old Virgin" and "Knocked Up."

ü **Nick Park (1958)** - Animator and director known for creating the characters Wallace and Gromit.

ü **Ryan Carnes (1982)** - Actor recognized for his roles in TV series "Desperate Housewives" and "General Hospital."

ü **Lindsay Price (1976)** - Actress known for her roles in TV series "Beverly Hills, 90210" and "Lipstick Jungle."

ü **Noel Clarke (1975)** - British actor, director, and writer known for "Kidulthood" and "Doctor Who."

December 7th

- **Ellen Burstyn (1932)** - Academy Award-winning actress known for her roles in "The Exorcist" and "Requiem for a Dream."

- **Tom Waits (1949)** - Singer-songwriter, musician, and actor known for his distinctive voice and eclectic music.

- **Emily Browning (1988)** - Actress recognized for her roles in "Sucker Punch" and "American Gods."

- **Jennifer Carpenter (1979)** - Actress known for her role in TV series "Dexter."

- **Nicholas Hoult (1989)** - Actor recognized for his roles in "About a Boy" and the "X-Men" film series.

December 8th

- **Kim Basinger (1953)** - Academy Award-winning actress recognized for her roles in "L.A. Confidential" and "Batman."

- **Teri Hatcher (1964)** - Actress known for her roles in TV series "Lois & Clark: The New Adventures of Superman" and "Desperate Housewives."

- **Ian Somerhalder (1978)** - Actor recognized for his roles in TV series "Lost" and "The Vampire Diaries."

- **Nicki Minaj (1982)** - Rapper, singer-songwriter, and actress known for her influential music.

- **Sam Hunt (1984)** - Country music singer-songwriter known for hits like "Body Like a Back Road."

December 9th

- **Kirk Douglas (1916)** - Legendary actor known for his roles in "Spartacus" and "Paths of Glory."

- **Judi Dench (1934)** - Academy Award-winning actress known for her roles in "Shakespeare in Love" and the James Bond films.

- **Simon Helberg (1980)** - Actor recognized for his role in TV series "The Big Bang Theory."

- **Kara DioGuardi (1970)** - Songwriter, singer, and former judge on "American Idol."

§ **Felicity Huffman (1962) -** Actress known for her roles in TV series "Desperate Housewives" and "Transamerica."

December 10th

v **Kenneth Branagh (1960) -** Actor, director, and filmmaker known for his adaptations of Shakespeare plays.

v **Raven-Symoné (1985) -** Actress and singer known for her roles in TV series "The Cosby Show" and "That's So Raven."

v **Emmanuelle Chriqui (1975) -** Actress recognized for her roles in TV series "Entourage" and "The Mentalist."

v **Michael Clarke Duncan (1957) -** Actor known for his roles in "The Green Mile" and "Armageddon."

v **Susan Dey (1952) -** Actress recognized for her role in TV series "The Partridge Family."

December 11th

Ø **Hailee Steinfeld (1996) -** Actress and singer recognized for her roles in "True Grit" and "Pitch Perfect 2."

Ø **Mos Def (Yasiin Bey) (1973) -** Rapper, actor, and activist known for his influential music.

Ø **Teri Garr (1947) -** Actress known for her roles in "Young Frankenstein" and "Tootsie."

Ø **Rey Mysterio (1974) -** Professional wrestler.

Ø **Rider Strong (1979) -** Actor recognized for his role in TV series "Boy Meets World."

December 12th

ü **Mayim Bialik (1975) -** Actress recognized for her roles in TV series "Blossom" and "The Big Bang Theory."

ü **Jennifer Connelly (1970) -** Academy Award-winning actress known for her roles in "A Beautiful Mind" and "Requiem for a Dream."

ü **Bob Barker (1923) -** Television personality and former host of "The Price Is Right."

ü **Sheila E. (1957) -** Musician and percussionist known for her work with Prince.

ü **Frank Sinatra (1915)** - Legendary singer and actor known as "The Voice" and "Ol' Blue Eyes."

December 13th

·   **Taylor Swift (1989) -** Pop and country music singer-songwriter known for her chart-topping hits.

·   **Jamie Foxx (1967) -** Academy Award-winning actor known for his roles in "Ray" and "Django Unchained."

·   **Christopher Plummer (1929) -** Academy Award-winning actor known for his roles in "The Sound of Music" and "Beginners."

·   **Steve Buscemi (1957) -** Actor and director recognized for his roles in "Fargo" and "Reservoir Dogs."

·   **Dick Van Dyke (1925) -** Actor known for his roles in "Mary Poppins" and "The Dick Van Dyke Show."

December 14th

o **Vanessa Hudgens (1988) -** Actress and singer recognized for her roles in the "High School Musical" film series.

o **Tori Kelly (1992) -** Singer-songwriter known for her powerful vocals and R&B music.

o **Nostradamus (1503) -** French astrologer, physician, and seer.

o **Miranda Hart (1972) -** British comedian, actress, and writer.

o **Patty Duke (1946) -** Academy Award-winning actress known for her roles in "The Miracle Worker" and TV series "The Patty Duke Show."

December 15th

§ **Don Johnson (1949) -** Actor known for his roles in TV series "Miami Vice" and "Nash Bridges."

§ **Adam Brody (1979) -** Actor recognized for his role in TV series "The O.C."

§ **Michelle Dockery (1981) -** Actress known for her role as Lady Mary Crawley on TV series "Downton Abbey."

§ **Tim Conway (1933) -** Comedian and actor known for his work on "The Carol Burnett Show."

§ **Helen Slater (1963) -** Actress recognized for her role as Supergirl in the 1984 film.

December 16th

v **Krysten Ritter (1981) -** Actress and musician recognized for her roles in TV series "Breaking Bad" and "Jessica Jones."

v **Benjamin Bratt (1963) -** Actor known for his roles in TV series "Law & Order" and "Miss Congeniality."

v **Billy Gibbons (1949) -** Musician and lead guitarist of the rock band ZZ Top.

v **Miranda Otto (1967) -** Australian actress known for her roles in "The Lord of the Rings" and "Chilling Adventures of Sabrina."

v **Jane Austen (1775) -** English novelist known for classic works like "Pride and Prejudice" and "Sense and Sensibility."

December 17th

Ø **Sarah Paulson (1974) -** Actress recognized for her roles in TV series "American Horror Story" and "The People v. O.J. Simpson."

Ø **Milla Jovovich (1975) -** Actress and model known for her roles in the "Resident Evil" film series.

Ø **Bill Pullman (1953) -** Actor recognized for his roles in "Independence Day" and "Spaceballs."

Ø **Manny Pacquiao (1978) -** Professional boxer and politician.

Ø **Laurie Holden (1969) -** Actress known for her role in TV series "The Walking Dead."

December 18th

ü **Brad Pitt (1963) -** Academy Award-winning actor known for his roles in "Fight Club" and "Inglourious Basterds."

ü **Katie Holmes (1978) -** Actress recognized for her role in TV series "Dawson's Creek" and films like "Batman Begins."

ü **Christina Aguilera (1980) -** Pop singer known for hits like "Genie in a Bottle" and "Beautiful."

ü **Ray Liotta (1954)** - Actor known for his roles in "Goodfellas" and "Field of Dreams."

ü **Stone Cold Steve Austin (1964)** - Professional wrestler and actor.

December 19th

· **Jake Gyllenhaal (1980)** - Academy Award-nominated actor known for his roles in "Brokeback Mountain" and "Nightcrawler."

· **Alyssa Milano (1972)** - Actress recognized for her roles in TV series "Who's the Boss?" and "Charmed."

· **Cicely Tyson (1924)** - Emmy and Tony Award-winning actress known for her roles in "Sounder" and "The Autobiography of Miss Jane Pittman."

· **Richard Hammond (1969)** - Television presenter known for co-hosting "Top Gear" and "The Grand Tour."

· **Criss Angel (1967)** - Illusionist, magician, and performer.

December 20th

o **Jonah Hill (1983)** - Actor and filmmaker known for his roles in "Superbad" and "Moneyball."

o **David Cook (1982)** - Singer-songwriter and winner of the seventh season of "American Idol."

o **Irene Dunne (1898)** - Actress known for her roles in "Cimarron" and "The Awful Truth."

o **Bob Morley (1984)** - Australian actor recognized for his role in TV series "The 100."

o **John Spencer (1946)** - Actor known for his role as Leo McGarry on TV series "The West Wing."

December 21st

§ **Samuel L. Jackson (1948)** - Academy Award-nominated actor known for his roles in "Pulp Fiction" and the "Star Wars" prequels.

§ **Jane Fonda (1937)** - Academy Award-winning actress known for her roles in "Klute" and "Coming Home."

§ **Kiefer Sutherland (1966)** - Actor recognized for his role as Jack Bauer in TV series "24."

§ **Ray Romano (1957) -** Comedian and actor known for his role in TV series "Everybody Loves Raymond."

§ **Chris Evert (1954) -** Former professional tennis player and multiple Grand Slam champion.

December 22nd

v **Meghan Trainor (1993) -** Singer-songwriter known for her pop and doo-wop-influenced music.

v **Ralph Fiennes (1962) -** Academy Award-nominated actor known for his roles in "Schindler's List" and the "Harry Potter" series.

v **Jordin Sparks (1989) -** Singer-songwriter and winner of the sixth season of "American Idol."

v **Hector Elizondo (1936) -** Actor recognized for his roles in films like "Pretty Woman" and "The Princess Diaries."

v **Diane Sawyer (1945) -** Journalist and former anchor of ABC's "World News."

December 23rd

Ø **Susan Lucci (1946) -** Actress known for her role as Erica Kane on TV series "All My Children."

Ø **Carla Bruni (1967) -** Singer-songwriter and former First Lady of France.

Ø **Corey Haim (1971) -** Canadian actor known for his roles in "The Lost Boys" and "License to Drive."

Ø **Holly Madison (1979) -** Television personality and former Playboy Playmate.

Ø **Chet Baker (1929) -** Jazz trumpeter and vocalist.

December 24th

ü **Ryan Seacrest (1974) -** Television host, producer, and radio personality known for hosting "American Idol."

ü **Ricky Martin (1971) -** Puerto Rican singer, actor, and author known for hits like "Livin' la Vida Loca."

ü **Stephenie Meyer (1973) -** Author known for the "Twilight" series of vampire-themed novels.

ü **Lemmy Kilmister (1945) -** Musician and founder of the rock band Motörhead.

ü **Ava Gardner (1922)** - Actress known for her roles in "The Killers" and "The Night of the Iguana."

December 25th

·   **Annie Lennox (1954)** - Singer-songwriter known for her work as part of the duo Eurythmics.

·   **Justin Trudeau (1971)** - Prime Minister of Canada.

·   **Sissy Spacek (1949)** - Academy Award-winning actress known for her role in "Coal Miner's Daughter."

·   **Helena Christensen (1968)** - Model and photographer.

·   **Humphrey Bogart (1899)** - Legendary actor known for his roles in "Casablanca" and "The Maltese Falcon."

December 26th

o **Jared Leto (1971)** - Actor and musician known for his roles in "Dallas Buyers Club" and fronting the band Thirty Seconds to Mars.

o **Kit Harington (1986)** - British actor recognized for his role as Jon Snow on TV series "Game of Thrones."

o **Steve Allen (1921)** - Comedian, musician, and the first host of "The Tonight Show."

o **Eden Sher (1991)** - Actress known for her role in TV series "The Middle."

o **Mao Zedong (1893)** - Founding father of the People's Republic of China and political leader.

December 27th

§ **Emilie de Ravin (1981)** - Australian actress recognized for her roles in TV series "Lost" and "Once Upon a Time."

§ **Salman Khan (1965)** - Indian actor and film producer.

§ **Hayley Williams (1988)** - Singer-songwriter and lead vocalist of the band Paramore.

§ **Bill Goldberg (1966)** - Professional wrestler and actor.

§ **Marlene Dietrich (1901)** - German-American actress and singer known for her film roles.

December 28th

v **John Legend (1978)** - Singer-songwriter known for hits like "All of Me" and "Ordinary People."

v **Denzel Washington (1954)** - Academy Award-winning actor known for his roles in "Training Day" and "Glory."

v **Maggie Smith (1934)** - Academy Award-winning actress recognized for her roles in "Harry Potter" and "Downton Abbey."

v **Sienna Miller (1981)** - Actress recognized for her roles in "Factory Girl" and "American Sniper."

v **Joe Manganiello (1976)** - Actor known for his roles in TV series "True Blood" and "Magic Mike."

December 29th

Ø **Jude Law (1972)** - Actor known for his roles in "The Talented Mr. Ripley" and the "Sherlock Holmes" films.

Ø **Jon Voight (1938)** - Academy Award-winning actor known for his roles in "Midnight Cowboy" and "Coming Home."

Ø **Alison Brie (1982)** - Actress recognized for her roles in TV series "Community" and "GLOW."

Ø **Jane Levy (1989)** - Actress known for her roles in TV series "Suburgatory" and "Evil Dead."

Ø **Mary Tyler Moore (1936)** - Actress known for her roles in "The Mary Tyler Moore Show" and "The Dick Van Dyke Show."

December 30th

ü **LeBron James (1984)** - Professional basketball player and four-time NBA champion.

ü **Ellie Goulding (1986)** - Singer-songwriter known for her pop and electronic music.

ü **Tiger Woods (1975)** - Professional golfer and one of the most successful players in history.

ü **Kristin Kreuk (1982)** - Actress recognized for her roles in TV series "Smallville" and "Beauty and the Beast."

ü **Meredith Vieira (1953)** - Television personality and former host of "Who Wants to Be a Millionaire."

December 31st

- **Val Kilmer (1959) -** Actor known for his roles in "Top Gun" and "Batman Forever."

- **Anthony Hopkins (1937) -** Academy Award-winning actor known for his roles in "The Silence of the Lambs" and "The Remains of the Day."

- **Donna Summer (1948) -** Iconic singer known as the "Queen of Disco."

- **Bebe Neuwirth (1958) -** Actress recognized for her roles in TV series "Cheers" and "Frasier."

- **Psy (1977) -** South Korean singer and rapper known for his viral hit "Gangnam Style."

Conclusion

As we come to the end of our journey through the calendar, exploring the lives of iconic individuals who share your birthday, take a moment to reflect on the significance of these connections. The stories we've uncovered span centuries, cultures, and fields of endeavor, reminding us that our birthdays are not just personal milestones, but threads woven into the larger fabric of human history. "More than Balloons: Your Celebrity Birthday Buds?" has allowed us to stand on the shoulders of giants, to see the world through the eyes of visionaries, and to appreciate the diverse contributions that have shaped our world. These shared birthdays serve as a testament to the power of the human spirit to inspire, create, and innovate.

Perhaps you've discovered a newfound connection to a historical figure who resonates with your passions, or maybe you've been inspired by the resilience and determination of individuals who overcame adversity to achieve greatness. Whether you share a birthday with a scientist who unlocked the mysteries of the universe, an artist who captured the essence of human emotion, or a leader who championed equality and justice, their stories are now a part of your own narrative.

As you blow out the candles on your next birthday cake, remember that you're not just celebrating another year of life; you're celebrating the legacy of those who came before you, the dreams you hold for the future, and the remarkable journey that is uniquely yours. You're a part of a constellation of individuals, each contributing their own light to the tapestry of existence. In the grand tapestry of time, we are each a thread woven into a larger narrative, and our birthdays serve as milestones that mark our place in that narrative. May this book continue to inspire you to embrace your individuality while recognizing the shared human experience that unites us all.

So, here's to the extraordinary individuals who've shared your birthday – the trailblazers, the creators, the leaders, and the dreamers. Here's to the connections that bridge the gap between past and present, reminding us that our lives are interconnected in ways that stretch beyond the confines of time and space. As you close the final pages of "More than Balloons: Your Celebrity Birthday Buds?" may you carry forward a sense of wonder, curiosity, and appreciation for the stories that have shaped you and the stories you have yet to create. After all, the journey of discovery is ongoing, and every day is an opportunity to add your own chapter to the story of humanity.

Happy reading, happy exploring, and above all, happy celebrating the remarkable individuals who share your birthday!